THE MIRACLE OF PRAYER

These stories are published because the readers of Alexander Lake's *YOUR PRAYERS ARE ALWAYS ANSWERED* requested it. Many of them told how that book had changed their lives—inspired them, renewed their faith in God, encouraged them to "try again," brought the sunlight of hope into the dark places of their souls, showed the way to physical and mental healing, and in a surprising number of instances, changed poverty to prosperity.

The author chose these true stories from more than two thousand he has collected during forty years. The result is a comforting volume of faith and reassurance for every reader's mood—a shining beacon guiding hearts to God through prayer.

CHOICE BOOKS
THE BEST IN FAMILY READING
P. O. Box 706
Goshen, IN 46526
We Welcome Your Response

YOU NEED
NEVER
WALK ALONE

Alexander Lcke

 PORTAL WARNER PRESS Anderson, Indiana

*Dedicated to
Dr. Franz J. Horch
and Maria*

Some of the stories in this book have appeared in the magazines *Good Business* and *Science of Mind*.

YOU NEED NEVER WALK ALONE

A PORTAL BOOK
Published by Pyramid Publications for Warner Press, Inc.,
by arrangement with Simon and Schuster, Inc.

Third printing February, 1974

Library of Congress Catalog Number: 59-7585

ISBN: 0-87162-143-6

Printed in the United States of America

PORTAL BOOKS are published by Warner Press, Inc.
1200 East 5th Street, Anderson, Indiana 46011, U.S.A.

Publisher's Note

Every story in this book is true. Names and descriptive facts have been altered in some instances to protect the privacy of the persons involved.

CONTENTS

HOW THIS BOOK CAME TO BE WRITTEN

THIS SECOND VOLUME of true answers to prayer stories is published in response to hundreds of written requests for it from readers of the first volume, *Your Prayers Are Always Answered*. The letters came from forty-nine states; Canada, Mexico, Japan and seven European countries—particularly England, Switzerland and Spain.

Many of the letters told of how *Your Prayers Are Always Answered* changed the lives of the writers—inspired them, renewed their faith in God, encouraged them to "try again," brought the sunlight of hope into the dark places of their souls, showed the way of faith to physical and mental healings, and in a surprising number of instances, changed poverty to prosperity.

The letters came from persons in all walks of life—congressmen, bankers, industrialists, writers, artists, movie and television stars, magazine editors, physicians, ministers, scientists, working men and women, members of the armed forces, inmates of several prisons, hospital patients.

In most cases, the subjects of the stories in *You Need Never Walk Alone* were suggested by letter writers who were seeking help in solving special problems. I spent a great deal of time going through the more than two thousand true answers to prayer that I've collected during forty years, and chose the ones herein, believing them to be the most inspiring.

I hope I've chosen well.

Smith River, California   A. L.
1958

WHEN I WAS a boy, the family spent the summer months on a farm Near Mishawaka, Indiana. One of our neighbors was an old lady named Tabitha Emerson. I loved to visit Auntie Tabitha, not so much for the sugar-coated cookies she kept in a crockery jar on a low shelf in the kitchen, as for her delightful stories and her happy knack for explaining things so a kid could understand. Auntie Tabitha was kindly, generous and wise. She wore her silver hair pulled tight across her ears and fastened in a twisted bun at the back. She dressed neatly in gray, and invariably wore a pink-and-white checked apron. My mother—a Canadian—spoke of Auntie Tabitha as a "gentle, bonny body."

One afternoon when I called on Auntie Tabitha, her nephew—about twenty-five, and from South Bend—was there. I entered the house just in time to hear Auntie say:

"You mustn't become impatient with God, Freddie. And you mustn't say that praying does no good. Perhaps before you ask other blessings of God, you ought to pray for patience."

"When I pray for something, Aunt Tabitha," Freddie said, "I pray because I want it right now, and I never pray for anything that I think isn't right. So why should God make me wait?"

"You're a good man, Freddie, and I don't know why your answers are slow in coming. I assume, though, that you're not ready for the answers."

"Well, what good is prayer if it brings things you need after the need has gone by?"

"Freddie, Freddie," Aunt Tabitha chided, "you've always been in too much of a hurry. Do you remember

9

when you used to visit me as a little boy, in early summer before apples were ripe? Remember how I used to warn you not to eat those hard, green little apples? And how you sometimes disobeyed, and ended up with a good old-fashioned stomach-ache?"

"I remember," Freddie said. "And you used to frighten me by calling plain stomach-ache 'cholera morbus.'"

Auntie Tabitha smiled in recollection, then said: "Well, you still seem to be the same Freddie—just can't wait for things to work out. It strikes me your prayer trouble, young man, is that you want God's answers green, and He wants you to have them ripe."

You Need Never Walk Alone

ONE DAY ABOUT THREE YEARS AGO A BUSINESSMAN IN Coquille, Oregon, told me a depressing story about his financial situation. When I suggested that prayer might help him, he said:

"It would, I think, if I had the faith of Frank Conliffe."

"Who's Frank Conliffe?" I asked.

"I buy my office supplies from Frank," he said. "He comes through here about once a month—has an office-equipment business at Coos Bay. For sixteen years, both of Frank's legs were paralyzed, but with God's help, he rose above his handicap. Today he not only walks, but covers two hundred miles of the Pacific Northwest Coast country each month in his car—calling on prospects and customers. He's a cheerful, helpful, confident fellow."

From time to time I heard more of Frank Conliffe from his customers and friends along Highway 101. At the northern end of his territory—Florence, Oregon—a customer said:

"A polio attack at the age of five months left Frank —as the doctors said—'hopelessly paralyzed from the waist down.' Today, although he walks a bit awkwardly, Frank's as nimble as a bush rabbit."

A woman of Harbor, Oregon—the southern extremity of Frank's territory—told me she'd talked to Frank for more than half an hour before realizing he was wearing a brace on one leg. "He doesn't *act* as if he were crippled, you see," she said. "He gives the impression of being a perfectly normal, healthy man. We always enjoy his calls, and my store seems a cheerier place after he's been here."

From persons in the Oregon towns of Gold Beach, Port Orford, Bandon, North Bend, Reedsport and Gardiner, I got other bits of Frank Conliffe's story. The more I heard, the more I wanted to write it. It was two years before I met Frank, and when I told him I wanted to interview him and write about him, he was genuinely surprised. "Why, I've done nothing worth writing about," he said.

"Your story's been an inspiration to many others," I said.

"Well, I don't understand that. I don't see . . ."

"You were paralyzed—now you walk. You were poor—now you've a prosperous business. You . . ."

"Well, yes—that's true," he interrupted. "But all that I am—all that I have—came from God."

"That's exactly it," I said. "That's the story I want."

"But all I did was to pray," Frank said. "Anyone can pray."

I realized that Frank Conliffe didn't understand how rare and how impressive his story was. Whenever he needed help, he simply asked God for it—and got it. To Frank, that seemed as natural as breathing. So, to get the story from him, I tried something like the Ralph Edwards "This Is Your Life" approach:

"Your parents, Frank," I began, "are Frederick and Mary Conliffe. You were born in Los Angeles, in 1921. When five months old, you were stricken with polio and became paralyzed from the waist down. Doctors wanted to put you in a cast, but your mother, after praying about it, said:

" 'I don't feel that God wants these dear little legs buried in cold, rigid plaster of Paris.' "

"That's right," Frank said. "And I'm fortunate to have a mother who prays. Doctors say now that if I'd been put in a cast, I'd never have walked."

"And your mother began treating you with massage and hot compresses?"

"Yes, she did. She was using the Sister Kenny treatment, although at that time we'd never heard of Sister Kenny. Mother 'discovered' the treatment through prayer."

"Your mother continued those treatments for a long, long time. Am I right?"

"Yes, she did—for sixteen years. They were long, sometimes discouraging, years, but my mother's faith was kept strong by prayer—and she taught me to pray, too."

I glanced at my notes. "And because you were unable to attend public school, you were taught at home by visiting teachers from the state educational facility for handicapped children?"

"Yes. Teachers came to our home twice each week, heard my lessons and assigned my studies for the next visit. But funds for that state educational program ran out shortly after my sixteenth birthday, so my formal education stopped there. By that time, my left leg was nearly normal, and I could have gone to public school, but instead I decided to take a job on a weekly newspaper—janitor, errand boy, type distributor, press washer—anything and everything. I know now that I took that job to overcome fear."

"Fear?"

"Fear of going out into the world and meeting it head on. It's easy, you know, for handicapped persons to think of themselves as cripples. When I felt I might be developing such an attitude, I prayed about it—prayed that God would keep me from thinking of myself as less than normal. An answer to that prayer came strong and clear—a thought that rang in my heart—that still rings clear: No man is a cripple unless his spirit is crippled."

Frank's look was earnest. "If there's to be hope for others in the telling of my story," he said, "I think it must come from the certainty that our individual spirits are part of God's spirit. When our spirits and God's spirit are in harmony, there's nothing but good for us. Physically, let's say, I'm somewhat 'different' than most, yet I've never found a job that other men of my weight and build can do—I weigh one hundred and thirty pounds—that I've not been able to do. I wear a brace on one leg, as you know—a completely useless leg. Yet after leaving the newspaper job, I was a house painter."

"You didn't climb ladders, though, of course."

"I certainly did," Frank grinned. "I climbed ladders everywhere—awkwardly, but successfully. I did my day's work as efficiently as other painters did theirs. God has never failed to give me confidence and strength."

"You had no fears of falling?"

"None. I knew God was protecting me."

"As simple as that!" I said.

"Yes, as simple as that." Frank hesitated a moment,

then said: "Don't you think it's a bit presumptuous for me to talk so much about myself?"

"There are so many, Frank, who don't know how to pray."

"Yes, that's true," he said. "Maybe you're right."

"Your house-painting job ended when you moved from California to Oregon. Your family settled in Coos Bay. What happened then?"

"I got a job in a pulp mill, wrapping and tying four-hundred-pound bales of pulp. The bales came along on a conveyor belt—came so fast that I seldom had a moment to relax during the ten-hour day. Believe me, that was plain, hard work—and boring, to boot. I was often so weary that I thought I'd drop, but day after day, week after week, month after month, I slogged away at those bales. It was prayer alone that enabled me to carry on. My fellow workers knew, of course, that I depended on God for strength and courage. I felt I couldn't let them down, nor God, nor myself. I stuck with that job until God sent me another, and then I quit with an easy conscience, for I knew that none of my 'normal' fellow workmen had done more, or better work, than I."

"And the new job?"

"Well, a man named Werner owned an office-equipment business in Coos Bay, and one day he offered me a job learning to repair typewriters and other office machines. At the pulp mill, I'd been earning fifty-one dollars a week. Mr. Werner offered me seventeen dollars a week. For some time, I'd been praying that God would open a way for me to learn a trade—something on which I could build permanent, constructive security. I felt the Werner job might be it—but seventeen dollars a week!

"For the next few days and night, I worried about what would happen if I took Mr. Werner's job, then found I couldn't pay off obligations that I'd contracted. The longer I worried, the greater my fear became. After all, I *was* handicapped, I told myself. Security meant more to me than to men with two good legs. Naturally, having begun to think negatively, it wasn't long before I was having quite a time feeling sorry for myself.

"But the habit of praying is strong. As I continued to pray, I began to realize that after all God had done for me through the years, I was doubting Him. I felt shame and remorse, and prayed for forgiveness. Almost before my prayer had ended I felt as if a kindly voice said:

" 'You asked Me for security, and I've sent you the Werner job. Accept it, my child, and have faith.'

"So I went to work for Mr. Werner, and I not only learned to live on seventeen dollars a week, but was able to save some money. Learning how to economize, to spend carefully and intelligently, came in handy in days to come. I'm now convinced that when God directs, *everything that occurs* is for some good purpose —holds some lesson to be learned. There were lots of problems on the new job, but prayer saw me through, and I must have done well, for one day Mr. Werner said to me:

" 'I think you're ready now, Frank, to buy the repair end of this business. You're young, efficient, conscientious and frugal. You can take that end over and pay me out of your earnings.'

"I signed the papers and took over. And things worked out well. Whenever I was up against what seemed a hopeless situation, I took the problem to God, and *He always solved it.*"

"That's an inspiring story, Frank," I said. "Can you please sum it all up for me now? What's your condition today?"

"Well, about three years ago I bought Mr. Werner's entire business—store, dealerships, repair shop—

everything. And the business has increased so that I now employ two full-time repair men, and a woman who manages the store. I spend most of my time on the road—servicing customers."

"And selling."

"Well—no. That is, I seldom *try* to sell anything; I only give service. I like to feel that all machines purchased from me are always in first-class working condition. Of course, I make many sales, but I never sell a man an item that I don't believe he needs. In fact, I sometimes turn down orders because I'm certain the customer's business doesn't really require the particular machine he's set his heart on."

"Competitors?"

"I help them when I can."

"And the lesson you've learned?"

"I've learned that we must not try to direct God's plans, but must follow confidently where He leads. One must consciously place his hand in God's, with loving faith and thankfulness. I've learned that faith in God turns darkness into light, discord into harmony, handicaps into assets and failures into successes. Faith—simple, prayerful faith—is the answer."

GOD WORKS THROUGH men, and prayers are always answered.

Those words are from a letter to me from Bela H. Banathy, now of Monterey, California, who, in 1947, left his two infant sons Bela, Jr. and Laszlo with his sister in Budapest, because conditions in the refugee camp at Branau, Austria, where he worked as draftsman and preacher, were unfit for children.

In 1951, the Banathys came to Monterey where Bela, Sr. got a job teaching Hungarian at the Army Language School. Bela, Jr. and Laszlo remained in Hungary because the Communists had taken over, and refused the children permission to leave. The Banathys restored to prayer, and obstacle after obstacle—not the least of which was the United States immigration regulations—was overcome until finally, nine long years after they'd kissed their babies good-by, the family was reunited in San Francisco.

The Banathys, so free of resentment against wartime enemies, made a deep impression on me, and I began questioning other refugees—Russians, Germans, Jews, Dutch, Hungarians—all who came my way. I discovered a wonderful thing: Nine out of ten told me that they owed their present freedom to prayer. Only one out of ten held hatred in his heart for persecutors, although some had known the horrors of sadistic prison camps.

I interviewed Germans who'd fought against us. A few had retained their faith in God through years of bloodshed and terror.

It seems that out of the holocaust of war comes even stronger faith. An example of this is the miracle of J. C. A. Faber's story, The Cart—The Grain—and Prayer.

The Cart—The Grain—and Prayer

J. C. A. FABER, OF BLARICUM, HOLLAND, TRANSLATOR of books for publishers, has achieved a unique reputation because of his ability to "catch the spirit" of manuscripts, even the weirdly idiomatic manuscripts of some American writers.

Many consider this ability to sense the meaning of obscure manuscripts miraculous. One publisher explains it by saying: "Faber's secret is really a simple one—he prays about each manuscript."

If you suggest to Faber that such answers to prayer require a special kind of faith, he'll tell you the story of his garden cart—a sturdy vehicle that has been a garden fixture at Faber's home at 13 Matthijsenhout Road since Holland's terrible "Hungerwinter" of 1944.

"The cart," he says, "is an answer to prayer, and is proof that nothing is impossible with God, even though what you pray for may seem impossible to you. That's the lesson I learned during that winter of desperate hunger, and that's the lesson that this cart keeps fresh in my mind.

"During the winter of 1944, the fourth year of German occupation, all western and central Holland faced starvation. There was no food in the normal channels of supply, for occupation forces had commandeered all of it. What little garden produce we'd been able to raise had been consumed, and by early December, desperately hungry families were ranging farther and farther afield in search for food—an egg or a potato here, a handful of grain there.

"By the middle of December, my family and I had reached the point where we had to find food—or die. I knew that farmers in northeastern Holland had harvested fair crops, and I knew that thousands of the hungry from other parts of the country were invading those farm areas to beg or buy whatever wheat or other grain they could. I decided that I also would go in search of foodstuffs.

"I wasn't much worried about finding grain, for I knew that Dutch farmers would give every morsel they could spare from their meager hoards. My big problem was how to transport it after I got it. The invaders had taken everything of value from us—all of the good bicycles, carts, wagons, scrap metal—everything. I needed a cart strong enough to carry a box of grain when towed behind the old wreck of a bicycle that the Germans had not thought worth taking. From waste materials that I scavenged, I built a cart—a wobbly travesty of a cart. On the cart I fastened an old wooden trunk. Then I hitched the cart to the bicycle, stepped back and looked at the contraptions, and grew half sick with despair. The outfit would shake to pieces within ten kilometers—and I had more than two hundred kilometers to go!

"I had always been a religious man, but hardly a praying one. Now, however, facing the greatest trial of my life, I was, like Abraham Lincoln, 'driven to my knees because there was no other place to go.'

"I don't think I prayed aloud, but I cried with my heart: 'Dear God, I reject all fear and doubt. I place myself in Your hands. Please direct me on my journey, and bring me—and the grain that I know You will help me to find—safely home to my family again.'

"A brief thought came to me that in asking God to help me keep that funny old cart running, I was asking too much of Him. I quickly prayed for faith, and felt suddenly filled with quiet certainty that no matter what difficulties might arise on my journey, God would help me overcome them.

"My faith was still strong the next morning when, in the chill dark, I mounted my bicycle, and with the fantastic cart bouncing, shaking and squeaking behind me, set out on a one hundred-kilometer trip to Zwolle, a country town northeast of Blaricum.

"It was still dark when I came to Polderland, whose fertile, below-sea-level fields—fields that had added so much to Holland's flori-cultural fame—had been flooded by the invaders, and were now covered road-deep with ice and water.

"I saw no one on the lonely Polder Road, but when I came to higher ground, and the main highway to Zwolle, I was amazed to find the traffic as heavy as if it were an Amsterdam street. And such traffic! Hundreds of elderly people, pulling, hauling, pushing, tugging or towing the most outlandish conveyances—baby buggies, gocarts, handcarts, pushcarts, children's wagons, barrows—many so rickety that my pitiful conveyance seemed superb by comparison.

"Yes, this was a dull-eyed, haggard, gaunt horde of elderly people, because if younger persons were physically able to make the trek, the invaders considered them able to work, and promptly shipped them off to work projects in Germany. And I knew, of course, that most of the food-hunters had started out that morning with empty stomachs, even as I.

"That night I was fortunate enough to get a room in a small wayside hotel, but most of the other travelers slept in haylofts and haystacks, and slept hungry, to boot. I arrived in Zwolle the next afternoon, and as there was daylight left, I decided to push on, taking the road to Meppel. Why? I saw that few traveled that road, yet I seemed impelled to do so. I traveled doggedly, passing farms at which I might have gotten wheat had I stopped to ask. As I peddled along the heavy road, I prayed that God would let me know when I came to the right farm. It was almost dark when I noticed a small dwelling on a side road, and felt that this was the place to which God had directed me. I knocked on the door, and despite the clothing that made me look like a beggar, a sweet-faced, hard-working mother bade me enter. I told her my name. She called her husband, a warm-hearted man named Gerrit Bruggeman. They introduced me to their five children and to 'Grandpop.'

"None asked questions, but invited me to sit down with them to a simple but well-cooked meal. Goodness, how I ate! I was starving—and they understood. And after supper, Bruggeman, Grandpop and I drank ersatz coffee beside the fireplace while Mrs. Bruggeman prepared a bed for me in the loft.

"'Hard job peddling that cart, wasn't it?' Bruggeman asked.

"'Well, if I hadn't been so hungry . . .'

"'I know. You've come to the right place. We have no spare grain ourselves, but neighbors have just finished threshing. In the morning I'll send my boy Jan with you. You'll fill your box in no time.'

"'It seems strange there were so few food-hunters on this road,' I said.

"'Not many come this way—I don't know why. Why did you?'

"'I prayed.'

"'You did well to pray,' Bruggeman said. 'God always knows best.'

"After family worship beside the dying fire, we went to our beds. I fell into deep, dreamless sleep almost before I'd had time to thank God for bringing me safely this far on my journey.

"The next morning, Jan and I filled my box in no

time, filled it to the brim. I offered money to the farmers. All refused it. 'No, no,' they said. 'we do not take pay to help those less fortunate than ourselves.'

"The Bruggemans asked me to stay with them for a day or two to rest, but word came that the Germans intended closing the Yssel Bridge south of Zwolle. As it was impossible to return home by any other route, I hurried away before it would be too late.

"With the heavily loaded trunk, I had to push my bicycle instead of riding it, and this meant that at least four days would be required for the journey home. As I plodded along, steering as I walked, I began to worry about the closing of the Yssel Bridge, and hurried faster and faster.

"And then—within a kilometer or so of the bridge—both cart wheels collapsed!

"In a state bordering on shock, I stood gaping at the cart frame—flat on the ground. Why had God let this happen now, after blessing the journey up to this point? Why hadn't God let me at least cross the Yssel Bridge first? The bridge would now be permanently closed, and my whole journey had been in vain!

"Overwhelmed with a feeling that I'd been abandoned, I cried, 'God, why did You forsake me?'

"For some time, my sense of loss remained, and the anxieties of my family, so hopefully awaiting my return, seemed to crowd upon me. I stood there, not even seeing the other food-hunters streaming past—my mind asking the question 'Why? Why? Why?' over and over. Then I suddenly felt ashamed, for the answer came clear: I had let my old habit of worry take over. I had feared the closing of the bridge. I said:

" 'Renew my faith, God. Help me to break the evil habit of doubt; for I realize, Lord, it is a habit—a faith-destroying habit of my mind. Help me to never doubt again.'

"Slowly, a strange elation filled me. I *knew*—knew beyond all uncertainty—that God had permitted me to shed my habit of fearing, as Pilgrim had shed his burden at the Slough of Despond.

"A woman, a neighbor of mine from Blaricum, paused beside me with her hard-won load of provisions. 'I wish there were something I could do to help you, Mr. Faber,' she said, "but there isn't of course. I'll tell your wife this bad news when I get home.'

" 'No, please,' I said. "Tell her that I'll be home on schedule with the grain. Tell her that everything is all right.' I smiled at her and wished her a safe trip home. She looked startled, then puzzled as she trundled her load on down the road.

"For a while, I stood beside my useless cart, then noticing a farmhouse across a field, I walked toward it. A horse-drawn wagon left the barnyard, coming my way. I told the driver about my accident, and he said:

" 'I'll haul your box of grain as far as the bridge. They won't let me go farther than that.'

"At the Yssel Bridge, two soldiers climbed on the wagon, hefted my box and said: 'Ammunition!' They called to the corporal in charge of the bridge guards: 'Paul, here's a box of ammunition!'

"The corporal, scowling, came to look. I lifted the box lid, ran my hand through the grain and said: 'You see, Paul? Only wheat.'

" 'We're closing the bridge for good in a few minutes,' he said. 'Unload your wheat and set it beside the road here, then hurry across.'

" 'But I want to take my grain, Paul,' I said. 'We need it desperately. Can't you help me to get it across?'

" 'No,' he said shortly. 'We've other things to do.' He turned away. I prayed silently: 'Help me, God. Please help me.'

"Paul paused, seemed thoughtful for a moment, then

turned back to me and said, pointing: 'Why don't you take that cart that stands over there beside that stone wall?'

"I looked, and sure enough—there was a cart, the very cart that I now use in our garden. It was just the thing I needed. I said calmly: "That cart will do nicely. Will you ask your soldiers to help me load the box on it, Paul?'

"Paul frowned. The soldiers looked indignant. Suddenly Paul said: 'Come on, boys. Put the box on the cart for this man.' They did, and I quickly hitched the cart to my bicycle and hurried over the bridge. I was one of the last travelers to get across.

"Weary, but thankful and happy, I trundled my load along for a few kilometers when popping noises behind me caused me to turn and look back at my new cart. Wheel spokes, shrunken by weather, were loosening— some spokes falling from the wheel rims. But this time I did not feel dismayed. I stopped, looked the situation over and decided that several lengths of strong wire would solve the problems; I could tie the spokes in with wire. But where could I get wire?

" 'God,' I said softly, 'I need wire. Please direct me.'

"I then waited confidently, praying silently.

"After a while, feeling restless, I began pushing my box of grain more to the center of the cart. Something between the cart board and one side of my box of grain caught my eye—a small reel of wire. I did not even feel surprised. I wondered how the wire got there, finally decided that the last owner of the cart had put it there for just such an emergency as this.

"Thanking God for His care of me, I wired all spokes strongly. And when I had finished, there was no wire at all left over.

"I arrived at my home on schedule.

"And so, that is the story of my garden cart. Can you

wonder now that I have utmost faith in prayer? In the matter of my business of translating, I don't think of what God does for me as a miracle. To me, it is only a natural result of faith in God's goodness. I keep that faith at high level by prayer."

MOST OF THE year, my family and I live in a beach studio on Pelican Bay near the California-Oregon state line. There Mildred, my wife, and I write articles, stories, TV scripts and books—when we're not watching the constantly changing colors of the Pacific, or dawdling in the garden. The nearest town is Smith River, California, a hemlet of about three hundred population.

One day an agnostic Hollywood producer, who was visiting us, said: "Anybody can collect answers to prayers if he'll scour the world as you've done, but just try to find prayer-answers in isolated rural communities—like this one!"

"I'll bet I can find twenty miraculous prayer-answers within a radius of ten miles of this studio," I said.

"It's a bet," he said.

So I spent four days visiting neighbors—and came up with many wonderful answers-to-prayers stories, including the following inspiring story of Henry and Margaret Zelka—"Through You, God Blessed Us."

Through You, God Blessed Us

HENRY AND MARGARET ZELKA, BOTH IN THEIR FIFTIES, arrived in the hamlet of Smith River, California, from Oregon, in the early fall of 1955. They had little money, but by doing janitor work in stores and markets of nearby Brookings, Oregon, and Crescent City, California, they were able to begin making payments on equipment for the rug and upholstery cleaning business they intended to operate.

They rented an ancient two-story frame building, moved their belongings into the upstairs, used the barnlike lower story as a storage room, and rebuilt a large outside shack for use as a cleaning and drying room. When, on December 22, they were almost ready to open for business, floods hit northwestern California. Hundreds of homes were washed away and lower floors of hundreds of others were inundated. Receding waters left rugs, carpets, upholstered furniture, mattresses and bedding soggy messes of mud, sand and slime.

Filled with compassion for their unfortunate new neighbors, the Zelkas, instead of using the disaster as a means of making money, let it be known that they'd clean and restore rugs, carpets and bedding of those residents too flood-impoverished to pay *free of charge*.

Immediately, and for nearly two months, their days were devoted to this labor of love, and each night, after a hasty meal, they worked until midnight at their janitor jobs, which brought in little more than enough to purchase cleaning compounds and other essentials for the next day's free restoration session. To speed things, they obligated themselves to make monthly payments on additional equipment.

"We really took on more than we should have, I guess," Henry told me when I interviewed him, "and the amount of work was staggering. However, at bedtime when it seemed we were too worn out to continue another day, we'd kneel and pray for strength. And always, we'd awaken next morning refreshed, and eager to be up and doing."

The rush of free work dwindled gradually, but on February 4, 1957, more than a year after the floods had abated, there were still two or three rugs left uncleaned.

When the Zelkas went upstairs to their living quarters that evening, they enjoyed an early supper, then sat back in easy chairs to enjoy an hour of relaxation before driving fifteen miles to Brookings to sweep and mop the floor of a supermarket. To rest aching feet, Henry slipped off his shoes. They were both half dozing when Margaret said:

"Henry, I smell smoke."

As if those words were a signal, flames exploded into the room. The Zelkas raced for the stairway, reaching the open yard only seconds before the entire building became a monstrous torch. Within twenty minutes, walls and roof of the eighty-year-old redwood structure collapsed in an inferno of roaring fire.

Everything that the Zelkas had owned was destroyed —furniture, clothing, money, equipment—even Henry's shoes. The volunteer fire department, unable even to approach the burning building, successfully devoted efforts to saving buildings across the street.

Without coats or hats, Margaret and Henry—Henry in sox—stood behind the fire lines, as Henry said, "absolutely stunned."

"Kind neighbors took us in for the night," Margaret said, "but during those hours of darkness, Henry and I were in a state of semi-shock. We felt as if the world had disintegrated. One minute we'd been happy and secure; the next, all was gone. Lying there holding hands, we kept asking each other, 'Why? Why had God let this happen to us?' We'd tried so hard to do what is right."

"We prayed," Henry said, "but all we were able to ask was, 'Why? Why? Why?' And there seemed to be no answer.

"We were two stricken, dumfounded people," Henry went on. "We knew what had happened, yet were unable to grasp it yet. We couldn't really *think*— we only *felt*.

"Gradually it dawned on us that we alone were the cause of the catastrophe. I'd been a builder at one time; when I'd rented the place, I'd known that eighty-year-old redwood becomes as inflammable as tinder. I'd been an electrician in days gone by, and I'd known perfectly well that electric wiring done in a haphazard manner—not in accordance with the Fire Underwriters' Code—holds a constant threat of fire. I'd known these things—had even thought of them briefly when I'd made the deal for the building. But I'd pushed the warning thoughts from my conscious mind.

"I'd been further in error by installing a furnace in that 'firetrap'—as a member of the volunteer fire department called the building—without taking sufficient precautions against overheating of the inflammable walls. We never did find out whether it was defective wiring, or the furnace, that caused the fire. It might have been both. We found no clue among the ashes.

"God had, as Paul says in the first chapter of Second Timothy, given me a sound mind. My error, I decided, was that in accepting the risk of a holocaust, I'd not been thinking soundly. Right then I prayed: 'From now on, God, please help me to *think right*.'

"That prayer was answered even as it was spoken—for the phrase from Titus 3:5 came to my mind: . . . *according to His mercy He saved us*. He'd saved us! Saved our lives! We'd been bewilderedly moaning about the loss of our possessions instead of going to our knees and thanking God will full hearts that He'd spared us. We owed God our lives! That was a wonderful thought. He'd spared us—and surely for a purpose of His own.

"Well, from now on, our lives would be fully His. It was a joyous decision, and although we didn't have a single valuable worldly possession left, we suddenly felt rich in gratitude and love and opportunity to build anew under God's direction.

"That night at our bedside, Margaret and I put our future entirely in God's hands, and we dropped off to sleep feeling comforted and secure.

"The next morning, a new miracle began when we opened two letters that had come in the mail. Each contained one-dollar bills from unknown donors. The next day, the next and the next, the mail containing small sums of money increased, and at the end of two weeks, we'd received more than two hundred dollars. Most of these gifts of money were sent anonymously, but a few letters said in effect:

"You cleaned our rugs and upholstery without charge when *we* were down and out because of the floods. Through *you,* God blessed us. Now *we,* in our turn, do what we can for *you.*

"An insurance policy, one that we'd feared might not apply to a loss like ours, was paid, bringing us nearly five hundred dollars. The merchant from whom we'd bought equipment and appliances arranged easier payments for us and gave us further credit. Gifts of clothing, tools, lumber, pots, pans, dishes, bedding and furniture began arriving. Within days, we were able to rent a small house trailer and move in.

"We were amazed that so many helped without revealing who they were. Such kind, understanding people; they wanted no thanks. Time after time, Margaret and I repeated the words of Jesus from John 16:20: . . . *and ye shall be sorrowful, but your sorrow shall be turned into joy.*

"Three weeks after the fire we had almost as many possessions as we'd had before. True, we had no building to move into, but that problem, too, God solved for us.

"A farmer about a mile south of Smith River owned

a two-acre tract on the highway—a valuable location. In order to help us, he set a price of three thousand dollars—far below the market value. On the land was a good well, a concrete and galvanized-iron building exactly right for a cleaning and drying room. Power lines passed the door. If we could add just one more small building, the place would be ideal for our business. We didn't have the three thousand dollars, but we did have prayer.

"God answered again. And a real estate woman in Crescent City lent us the three thousand dollars. A legal transfer was made, and the new cleaning plant and homesite became ours—with payments so easy that they'll never be a problem.

"At a fantastically low price, a millowner sold us sufficient lumber for the additional small building we needed. Electric wire, water pipe and other needed items were donated—some of it by total strangers.

"And so, exactly forty-eight days after the fire, Margaret and I were in business again, and living in a modest but comfortable trailer home.

"We believe that God spared our lives for a purpose. It may be that He wishes us to carry on in our small sphere, just being living testimonies to His goodness. Or it may be that He has wider work for us to do. Whatever His plans for us may be, we'll prayerfully wait for Him to reveal them. And through prayer, from now on we'll *think right*."

THE TEACHING OF Christianity to many tribes of African natives is complicated by peculiarities of language and native thinking. One must be careful to not use words that violate long-established customs. For example: Among some Boran tribes, the word "blood" has a connotation of "unclean." On the other hand, to the Masai tribes, "blood" is the staff of life. Blood mixed with milk is the Masais' only food. Among the Somalis, there are no words for colors. One cannot say: "a red bird," "a green tree," etc. One says: "A bird the color of a wilderness poppy," or "a tree the color of grass after the rains."

Among some Congo tribes you do not ask: "To what tribe do you belong?" Instead, you inquire: "How do you dance?" Among the Pygmies, the word "snake" connotes evil. Among the Zulus, the word "snake" means "guardian spirit (elhose)." Among Pygmies, there's no single word that means "good." However, the word "river" has all the meaning of "good." In one sense "river" means "living water" or, as the Bible says: "the water of life."

In the following story, "gourd" not only means "heart," but also means "chest" and "soul."

The Gourd and the Good River

M'NINGI WAS A PYGMY CHIEFTAIN, WHOSE TRIBE STILL lives in the west-central area of the Congo's Great Rain Forest. When I first met M'Ningi in 1912, he was about forty-five years old, four feet two inches tall and weighed ninety-five pounds. He had yellowish-brown skin and a large head that was matted with kinky hair. His nose was broad, but not flat; his torso long and muscular and his legs short.

Of the twenty-nine Pygmy Chieftains of the Great Forest, M'Ningi was the only one who prayed to the Christian God. And because this was so, his tribe lived without war, without fear of mythical forest demons, without witchcraft.

Although M'Ningi was no larger than other men of his tribe, he was called M'Ningi—the Great One—because of his spirit, which was unique among the eighty thousand Pygmies of Africa.

When I asked M'Ningi how it happened that his tribe seemed always well fed, healthy and at peace with its neighbors, he answered in the language of the Bankuto:

"It is because I fill my gourd every morning with water from the Good River."

When he spoke the word "gourd," he placed his hand over his heart. When he said "the good river," he pointed to the sky. His statement meant that every morning he filled his heart from the river of good that flows down from Heaven.

M'Ningi's story was told partly in Bankuto, partly in Kiswahili, and partly in "The-Language-of-the-River"

—a sort of pidgin. I am letting him tell his story as nearly as possible in his own words. First, however, a bit of the background of the Pygmy peoples:

These "dwarfs" are believed to be Africa's and India's first inhabitants. Herodotus, the Greek historian, says that the African Pygmies' earliest home was the Libyan Desert. Painting of Pygmies were made in Egypt before 2600 B.C. The name "Pygmy" is from the Greek word *pugmaios*—a cubit (less than one yard) tall.

Century by century, the Pygmies retreated before the Negroes and the Hamites until at last they took refuge in the dense rain forests of Central Africa. Here they became nomads, moving from area to area as the animals—on which they lived—moved about. Pygmies, even to this day, do not acquire possessions. They erect no permanent homes, but at each resting place they build little huts from bent saplings. The walls and roofs are made with heavily leafed tree branches. The wealthiest Pygmy family I know owns only a small cooking pot, three used safety-razor blades, two empty tomato cans, a few glass baubles, several bows, two spears and about thirty arrows.

Writers have misstated that the Pygmies are slaves to nearby Negro tribes. The truth is that certain Bantu tribes have "adopted" Pygmy tribes that roam in their vicinity. The Bantus (Negroes) protect their Pygmy "wards" against exploitation, and supply them with vegetables in return for meat. Pygmies are great hunters—killing even elephants with their short spears and tiny arrows. The Pygmies surrender all ivory to their Bantu chiefdoms as a "hunting fee." The relationship between the "big people" and the "little people" is friendly, and mutually beneficial.

In fighting, Pygmies used poisoned darts, arrows and spears. The poison, made from caterpillars' entrails mixed with the sap of certain trees, is violent and deadly. However, when not interfered with, Pygmies are cheerful, kindly little folk. No parents dote more on their children; and like the young of almost all creatures, Pygmy babies are cute, lovable little rascals.

Until M'Ningi, in 1909, met my missionary father Dr. John G. Lake, he was a creature filled with fears. He lived in dread of white men, other Pygmy tribes, witchcraft and a host of imaginary devils. Although he and the men of his small tribe were adept with poisoned weapons, stronger tribes were constantly driving them from areas where game was plentiful. Consequently, his people often suffered from famine and from hunger-induced diseases. One morning, M'Ningi was ambushed by an enemy hunting party. Here's the way he told the story:

"The arrow of my enemy pierced my hand, and the blood ran out like froth. In ten breaths, the froth would reach my gourd (heart), and I would go to the Land-of-Meat-that-Grows-on-Trees (Happy Hunting Grounds), but I tied a *liana* (tourniquet) about the wrist, and the froth stood still in my veins. But my gourd grew empty of air and I fell down. Then I crawled under a bush, for I knew I would quickly go on the long journey to the Land-of-Meat. My enemy ran away.

"Then my flesh hurt and I screamed: 'Eeee! Eeee!' and a Big One (John G. Lake), a Talk-talk *bwana* (missionary) heard me, and he looked into the bush and saw me—and it was dark. (He'd been unconscious.)

"The Big One said: 'You will not go to the Land-of-Meat. You will return to your people and tell them about the God-that-is-Good.' Then he put his hands on my head and looked up to the Sky River and he said in Kiswahili:

" 'Take away this man's pain, O Baba, so that he will know that You are God.'

"And my hurt ran away. And I did not continue to cry: 'Eeee! Eeee!'

"Then the Big One said: 'Stand on your feet.'

"I said: 'It cannot be, for my bones are soft.'

"And the Big One put his hands on my legs and looked up to the Good River and said: 'Make him strong, O Baba, so he will know that You are God.'

"And I stood on my feet and walked. And the Big One went with me to my people.

"When my people saw me walking, they cried: 'Eyah! Eyah!' and they said: 'He is a dead one, yet he walks' (a ghost). Then they ran away. But I called: "Return, for this Big One's God is greater than the demons in the poison.'

"So they came—and fell on their faces before the Big One. And the Big One said: 'Stand!' and they stood. Then he said:

" 'My God loves the Pygmies. My God is Good. He has made a river above the clouds, and from the river flows a good water that makes demons cease to exist Each night you must empty your gourds of the angry things that bite the spirit like snakes. Then you must look up to the Good River and say: "O Baba, who is God, fill my gourd with Your Good Water that I may live in the day and in the night without snake thoughts." And God will fill your gourds, and you will be happy and will have plenty.'

"Then the Big One went away, for his porters came and found him. And he was gone. And we fill our gourds at the Good River until this day. And none has fought us since that time, and we have not been hungry.

"Truly, Baba is a good Baba, and His River is Good."

A HOLLYWOOD PRODUCER, who is planning a movie based on answered prayers, having read my collection of true prayer stories commented:

"The outstanding feature of these stories is that in every case *a prayer of thanks either preceded or followed the prayer of petition. Which reminds me of a little story I heard a minister tell in a small Methodist church in Indiana when I was a boy.*

"It seems that one morning the angels in Heaven who record the prayers of earthlings found their books becoming more and more unbalanced. Deciding to check, they called two husky angels, gave each a basket and told them to hurry down to Earth and gather up the prayers for that day. One angel was told to collect 'asking prayers.' The other was to collect 'thanking prayers.'

"That night, the angel who'd gone after 'asking prayers' fluttered into Heaven dead beat, his basket jam-packed with prayers. Shortly thereafter, the 'thanking prayer' collector whizzed in, with only one lone 'thanking prayer' rattling around in his basket.

"After reading these stories," the producer said, "I feel that a movie based solely on prayers of petition would be gravely lacking, indeed. I'm going to get busy and try to dig up some writers who can incorporate praise and thanksgiving into the script."

His remarks recalled to me an incident that happened years ago, while I was working as a reporter on the Spokane Chronicle. I interviewed an old lady named Prunella Morphy on her one hundredth birthday. When I asked the customary question: "To what do you credit your long life, Mrs. Morphy?" she replied:

"Prayers,—and that don't mean 'gimme' prayers."

"Exactly what are 'gimme' prayers, Mrs. Morphy?"

"Some folks are always asking God to 'gimme this' and 'gimme that.' Me, I always prayed 'thankee' prayers. You see, young fellow, I always been sprightly; my eyes have been good, always heard well, never had any miseries that amounted to much, always was able to keep the cows milkin', the chickens scratchin' and the potaty bugs off the potaties. I was always so busy workin' that I never had time to get too fat. I was always a great hand for sunrises, so gettin' up at the crack o' dawn every sunny day started the day out just right. When it rained, and there weren't no sun, it made me feel good to see the way my growin' vegetables stood up straight with their shoulders back.

"Truth to tell," Mrs. Morphy concluded, "if a body takes time to thank God for all the good things He's given him, he'll be so busy sayin' 'thankee' prayers that he won't need to be sayin' 'gimme' all the time."

Sweet Hour of Prayer

A SMALL FRAMED CARD ON A WALL OF THE RECEPTION room of Dr. Paul Kirby's New York City dental office read:

> ". . . Sweet hour of prayer
> That calls us from a world of care."

A receptionist, noting my interest in the card, smiled and said:

"Dr. Kirby says he owes every 'stick and stone' in

this business, to prayer. He hung that card there, hoping people would ask about it. He tells his story whenever possible."

When I said I'd like to hear the story, too, I was told that the doctor was rushing to catch up with his work because he was scheduled to leave on a trip. However, Kirby stepped out of his cubicle long enough to shake hands and to say he'd be glad to tell his story to me after he returned.

My publisher had already arranged for me to speak on "prayer" at three large churches in North Carolina, so a few days later I boarded a plane for Greensboro. Seating myself next to a window, I glanced at the passenger who had seated himself next to me—Dr. Kirby.

Here is the story that Kirby told as the plane creaked and shivered its way southward:

"I was brought up in an orphanage, in a backward part of Pennsylvania, and for almost seventeen years I was overworked and underfed. The orphanage—it was more like a poorhouse—was run by a red-bearded man named Kline. He was a stern man, and he frequently caned both boys and girls.

"We endured the whippings, but Kline's 'praying' was almost more than we could stand. The prayers always followed a caning, and consisted chiefly of instructions to God on how to punish children who got behind in their work, or who complained about the food. Long and tedious, his prayers did not end until he'd recited a full list of our shortcomings—and those were the only prayers we kids ever heard. We had no religious instructions of any kind, so even the little shavers decided that both God and Kline hated children. And I developed an antagonism toward prayer that stayed with me for many years.

"Among the thirteen other children in the orphanage

was a blue-eyed, flaxen-haired little girl named Martha, who was two years younger than I. And next to me, Martha was Kline's pet dislike—and she was whipped almost as often as I was.

"Until I was seventeen, I'd never had even fifty cents of my own. And then one day after some visitors had gone, I found a ten-dollar bill on the lawn. The next day, Martha and I ran away to Philadelphia and persuaded a minister to marry us. I immediately got work as a gas fixture assembler in a small shop on Ninth Street—six dollars a week for a twelve-hour day, six days each week. A light-housekeeping room, high under the eaves in an old house on Arch Street, cost us one dollar and fifty cents a week. That left four dollars and fifty cents, and we lived on that not only like kings —compared to our lives in the orphanage—but saved money. Very much in love, we would have been completely happy had it not been for our fear that Kline, whom we both hated, would find us and force us to go back.

"Not long ago I was looking through a little book of accounts that Martha had kept in those days. Sardines were five cents a can; Uneeda biscuits, five cents; a twenty-four ounce loaf of bread five cents; potatoes, two pounds for a penny. Wood and charcoal for the tiny cooking stove cost us twelve cents a week, we used the stove only for cooking, since heat from downstairs flowed into our room when the door was open. We bought secondhand clothes on South Street— and still managed to save about two dollars a week.

"One warm summer evening, to escape the stuffiness of our attic room, we strolled out into the comparative coolness of Market Street. A crowd at the entrance to an empty store attracted our attention and we paused to watch a white-jacketed 'painless' dentist extract a tooth from the mouth of a man seated on an ordinary kitchen chair. Holding the molar high so all could see it, he said:

" 'See, folks! Absolutely painless! Why? Because I injected a few drops of a magic painkiller, the greatest dental discovery of all time!' He helped the patient to his feet, patted him on the shoulder, told him to rinse his mouth with warm water when he got home, then asked:

"Who's next? Which of you wants to end toothache for all time?'

"Since I'd had a nagging toothache for weeks, this seemed the time to do something about it. 'How Much?' I asked.

"The dentist smiled. 'Would you pay five dollars?' he asked.

" 'Well . . .'

" 'Of course you would! But you don't have to. I'll end your tooth misery for just fifty cents. Step up quickly, please—others are waiting.'

"The crowd opened for me and I seated myself in the chair. A voice in the throng said: 'It's hypnotism, that's what it is!'

"The dentist held out his hand and I put fifty cents in it. He looked into my mouth and said:

" 'You've two very bad teeth; both should come out. Have you another half-dollar?'

"I gave him two quarters. He lifted a large syringe, poised it, jabbed the needle into my gums, pressed the plunger, withdrew the needle, spoke to his audience for two or three minutes, then said to me:

" 'Open your mouth.'

"I did. I'd have sworn his right hand was empty, but the forceps appeared like magic. In seconds, both teeth were out, and I'd felt nothing at all.

"Martha and I stayed to watch that dentist pull more than twenty teeth. As we strolled away, Martha said:

"Why, that man earned more than ten dollars while we stood there, Paul! Ten dollars in less than an hour!'

"'Someday, Martha,' I said impulsively, 'I'll be a dentist, too. I may even have an office of my own.'

"'Oh, darling! Do you think you ever could?—be a dentist, I mean. That would mean a home of our own someday, and a yard with flowers! Oh, Paul, do you really think you could?'

"'Sure,' I said, 'why not?'

"From that moment, dentistry was our dream, and we lived only for the day that dream would be realized. The next evening, we waited until the dentist had closed up shop, then I asked him how much he'd charge to teach me painless dentistry. He stared at me thoughtfully, and I thought he looked sick, or sad. He finally asked:

"'Do you drink?'

"'No, sir.'

"'Well, I do. And that's why I'm a pitchman, and why I'm chased by the police from pillar to post.' Then, after glancing from Martha to me several times, he said:

"'I'll teach you—for one hundred dollars.'

"'I could pay a dollar a week,' I said.

"He laughed. 'I've a better idea, my boy. Can you grow a mustache?'

"I thought he was making fun of me and I turned away angrily.

"'If you can grow a mustache, I'll teach you how to yank a tooth and how to inject the painkiller. And then you can make a pitch of your own. I'll make a good tooth puller of you, my boy. But I'll expect half of all that you make for—let's see—for two years.'

"Well, the man kept his word, and wearing a mustache that added years to my appearance, within two months I was making my first pitch in the small town of Port Deposit, Maryland, while Martha and the dentist

watched from the crowd. On the second night, the police ran me out of town—but not before I'd taken in
thirty-two dollars.

"During the next two years, Martha and I covered a
large part of the United States, and I pulled an estimated seven thousand teeth. When we'd saved eighteen
hundred dollars, we moved to Detroit, where I enrolled
in a small dental college, and Martha entered Cass High
School. And on the day after I received my diploma, I
became a full-fledged dentist in the Detroit branch of
the famed Painless Parker's pioneer dental chain.

"For three years, we worked hard and lived frugally,
and by the time Martha was graduated, we had about
five thousand dollars in the bank—enough, we decided,
to start our own dental practice. So we returned to Philadelphia, and after surveying several possible locations,
we chose a three-room suite on Eighth Street between
Market and Walnut. I figured that from the wealthy
Walnut area, I'd draw my chief income, and from the
poor folks across Market, I'd get mostly extractions and
cheap fillings.

"We bought supplies, equipment, a house and furnishings, and paid a total of forty-five hundred dollars
down, contracting to pay the balance in monthly payments of almost one thousand dollars—quite a large
obligation for those days, but we'd be able to meet it by
taking in only thirty-five dollars a day, seven days a
week.

"Patients were plentiful from the first hour we
opened; poor patients from the semislums on the other
side of Market. The wealthier folks from beyond Walnut didn't come near us. And even at that, we might
have made it if all of the patients had been able to pay
for the work done, but many couldn't.

"Martha was my assistant, and although we worked
almost without letup from early morning until late at

night, we were three hundred dollars short when our first month's payments fell due. We made it up within a week, but that left only three weeks to take in the second thousand dollars. And that second time we were two weeks late.

"Month by month we fell further and further behind —and our nerves and stamina began failing. It was work and worry, worry and work.

"We discussed quitting many times, but always decided to carry on just one more month. And then the day came at last when both the real estate people and our wholesaler demanded back payments due them within thirty days—or else.

"By then, of course, we'd long been aware that *true* prayer wasn't Kline's sort of prayer, yet we'd felt that we both had what it takes to succeed without help from anyone—even God. Now, however, despairing and humbled, we prayed many times.

"And nothing happened. The seemingly hopeless days dragged on.

"Then one morning one of our regular patients—an old physician named Brownlee, who'd spent most of his adult life working among the very poor—seated himself in the chair, looked from Martha to me, frowned and said:

" 'You two should take a vacation; you're sick people.'

" 'It's only strain and worry,' I said. 'And we'll be taking a permanent vacation in about three weeks. We're about to lose this business.'

" 'Well, maybe it's for the best,' Brownlee said. 'Sometimes health's more important than . . .'

" 'No,' I said, 'it's not for the best; it's the worst thing that could happen to us.'

" 'Well, I've lived a long time,' he said, 'and when I

come to an impasse of any kind, I pray. Have you two prayed about your problems?'

" 'Yes—and God hasn't answered our prayers.'

" 'But God *always* answers; that is, unless there's something unsettled between you and Him. *Is* there?'

" 'No,' I said.

" 'There's nothing that God would have you two do that you've left undone?'

" 'Nothing I know of. Is there, Martha? Now please, Doctor, let's get to your work; others are waiting.'

" 'Yes, I know. But listen: God is Love. He loves us. We must love Him. Do you both really *love* God?'

" 'Of course,' I said.

" 'Do you hate anyone?'

" 'No, of course not. We're not the hating kind. Except . . .' My words died as I pictured Kline. 'Well,' I said, 'there's *one* man—he did us great harm!'

" 'Forgive him.'

" 'Nonsense. That man—he—that man was a devil. He . . .'

" 'God is Love. You believe that, don't you?'

" 'Of course.'

" 'Hatred is evil. Isn't it?'

" 'Well, yes—I guess so.'

" 'You *know* so. How can you ask Love to come into hearts filled with hate? Stop hating that man.'

" 'Look here, Doctor,' I said. 'You can't just turn hate on and off like a faucet; nor love either, for that matter.'

" 'No, *you* can't—but God can. I suggest you two people kneel down and ask God to change that hatred into love. After that, you'll be able to expect that your prayers for God's direction in your lives will be heard. Be eager to pray. It's a sweet and good experience.'

"Nothing more was said then, while I worked on Dr. Brownlee's teeth. And I watched him silently as with smiling eyes and a nod, he left the office. It wasn't until hours later, after the last patient had gone, that Martha and I had time to talk. I said:

" 'I can't just stop hating Kline, Martha. Why—that hatred's carried me over some of the toughest spots. Often, when it's looked like I was beaten, I've said to myself: "Quit now, my boy—and *how* Kline will laugh!" I'd get so mad then that I'd whip the situation. But you know all this, Martha.'

" 'Yes, I know,' she said. 'We've hated for a lot of years, Paul. Still, I wonder . . . ? Well, let's go home now, dear.'

"Martha slept soundly that night, as usual, but I fumed and worried all through the dark hours. I tried to comfort myself by blaming Kline for all our troubles— including our impending bankruptcy. I got up at dawn, nerves raw and quivering. I was in a mean mood by the time I reached the office, and got meaner throughout the day. During a quiet spell toward evening, Martha said:

" 'You know, Paul, Mr. Kline doesn't *know* that we hate him.'

" 'But *we* know.'

" 'Yes. But who is our hatred hurting, after all?'

" 'Okay,' I said, 'forgive him—if you can.'

"At home that night we were both on edge a bit as we ate supper; neither of us seemed able to get Kline out of our minds. Martha went to the kitchen to tidy up; I sat with a newspaper—not understanding a word that I read. After a while Martha came through the dining room door, a dish towel in her hand.

" 'Paul,' she said, 'perhaps Mr. Kline was sad and lonely, sort of lost among all of us kids. Anyway, I can't feel hatred toward him any longer.' She came close and touched my cheek. 'Let's talk to God about it—now, Paul. Let's tell Him that we've both begun to forgive

Mr. Kline.' Then Martha knelt right there beside my chair. Somewhat rebelliously, I knelt down beside her.

"We knelt there for nearly an hour, and the only words spoken aloud were a whispered: 'Please, God,' from Martha. And a wondrous quieting of our spirits occurred, a feeling that we were beginning to *know* God. We'd found Someone who cared for us—Someone we could always trust and love.

"When we got to our feet, Martha, with tears of joy, came into my arms. 'Paul. Remember the hymn we heard once in that little church in North Dakota—'Sweet Hour of Prayer'?'

" '*This* hour has been sweet,' I said. 'You know, Martha, I'm no longer worried about our business. I feel whatever happens, will be for the best. Strange, isn't it?'

"A sense of exaltation stayed with us all evening, and hoping to know more about prayer, and about what God expected of us, we began reading the New Testament aloud to one another, taking turns. Those words of Jesus': *Love thy neighbor—love little children—love one another—walk in love—Love is of God—God is Love!*

" 'Poor Kline,' I said to Martha as she closed the Bible.

"Martha smiled. 'Looks like we might learn to truly love that man. Oh, Paul!'

"Next morning we went to work an hour earlier than usual, and we prayed there in the quiet waiting room; a custom we've followed ever since. Our 'sweet hour of prayer,' we call it."

Kirby stared down at the earth for a few minutes.

"I must hurry with the rest of the story. I'm getting off at Washington and we'll soon be there.

"On that very first 'sweet hour of prayer' morning, and only about an hour later," he continued, "the reception room was crowded with a group of obviously poor folks. One elderly woman was counting small change, hoping, apparently, that she had enough for whatever dental work she needed. My heart instantly went out to her. I called Martha aside and said impulsively:

" 'We've probably only three weeks of this practice left. Let's devote them to the poor—without charge.'

"Martha smiled. 'Okay, dear. Why not?'

"One of the patients that morning was a young man with a toothache. When he offered to pay, I said:

" 'Only if you can afford it.'

" 'What's this?' he asked, 'a gag?'

"I explained we were about to be closed out; that we were devoting the rest of the time to people who were unable to pay. He made some matter-of-fact comment and left.

"The next day the *Public Ledger* ran a short item about our free work, referring to us as the *Eighth Street Free Dental Clinic*. That young man was a reporter on the *Ledger*. And that did it!—the poor flocked to our offices, particularly old folks and children.

"Then a Walnut Street broker came one day, asked some questions and left. An automobile agency executive visited us, asked questions and left. A famous woman dress designer talked a long while with Martha one day, and seemed deep in thought when she left. And so it went for several days—more than twenty prominent Philadelphians investigated our practice.

" 'Then a few days later, our wholesaler telephoned that we could have as long as necessary to pay off our debt; we sold our equity in our home and added two rooms to our office to help handle the rapidly increasing number of well-to-do patients. These wealthy people enabled us to continue our free clinic indefinitely. And we were about to hire another dentist—were interviewing applicants, in fact—when city and county social services began taking over many of our needier patients.

"As you must have noticed the other day when we met, we've prospered greatly, for in God's right time, we moved our practice to New York City—and that daily hour of prayer remains our bulwark. We've learned that God is infinitely wise; that He *does* what's best. And because His love is in the hearts of each one of us, our own hearts desire only what is good."

ONE SUNNY MORNING in northern Transvaal, a missionary party consisting of the Reverends Duggan, White, Amm, Armstrong, Schwede and Lake (my father), holed up in a grass hut belonging to a native goat herder because they were being trailed by a lean male lion that was moaning with hunger. The beast was one they'd been warned about at Umluzi's kraal the day before—a man-eater that had killed one male native and two women.

Man-eaters are usually in a state of near-starvation, being too old and slow to prey on fast-moving antelope. Old and starving though they be, they still weigh more than four hundred pounds, and are fast enough to catch a running man in a couple of forty-foot jumps.

Like most missionaries, the party traveled without guns.

Afraid to attempt entry to the hut, the lion began circling it at a distance of about thirty yards, stopping from time to time to crouch. Facing the doorway, he switched his tail and indulged in short grunting moans. After about an hour of this, the lion's circle had decreased to about twenty yards, and the missionary party began to fear that one of them might soon become a meal for the determined animal.

The six missionaries finally knelt and asked God to protect them, remaining for several minutes on their knees. Abruptly, Schwede got to his feet and said:

"I believe that if that lion understood that we're on God's business, he'd go away. I'm going outside and tell him." Then he walked out into the open.

Seeing Schwede, the lion promptly crouched, snarled

and stiffened his tail—a sure sign he was about to spring. Schwede said:

"Go away. You're interfering with the work of God."

The lion lifted his hindquarters, tensed for the leap. Schwede said:

"In the name of Jesus Christ, go away," and took a step or two toward the threatening animal.

The lion lifted his upper lip, snarled and began backing.

Schwede stood still.

The lion backed a little more, then turned and stalked off with great deliberation until he got behind a bush. Finally he took off at a lope, stopping once behind another bush to peer back at Schwede over its top.

The last the party saw of the man-eater, he was disappearing among huge boulders at the top of a shallow hill.

When I interviewed Reverend Schwede, he told me that as he knelt after praying, he heard an inward voice say:

He shall call upon me, and I will answer him: I will be with him in trouble; I will deliver him, and honour him.

"It was God's promise," he said. "I accepted it and went out and told the lion to go on his way. He did."

"And you weren't afraid?" I asked.

"I was not afraid."

God Works in Wondrous Ways

WHEN I HEARD THE REMARK, "GOD AND BUSINESS DON'T mix," I invariably think of Abe Read who, with God's help, was not only able to conduct a hazardous business for almost forty years, but survived gloriously despite seemingly intolerable persecution. Read's sole source of religious instruction was his Bible. His strength and endurance came from God, through prayer. Here, briefly, is his story:

Mary, Abraham Read Virginlow's mother, wife of a Cornish coast smuggler, did all she could to bring her young son up in the love of God. Peyn Virginlow, the father, a hard-drinking, brutal man, forbade mention of God in his house. But Peyn was away most of the time, and during those periods mother and son spent hours praying, singing psalms and reading the Bible. Abraham was only ten when he joined the Band of Hope and pledged that he'd never touch liquor.

Mary died when Abraham was twelve, and the father forced his boy into a career of petty thievery, beating him when he protested. And so for two years Abraham pilfered from boats along the waterfront near Lowey. He was a month past fourteen when he ran away to sea, taking with him nothing but the clothes on his back and a small, dog-eared New Testament that had been his mother's.

Captain and crew of the West African coaster on which Abraham had sailed proved as godless as Peyn Virginlow, and because Abraham consistently refused to drink his daily ration of rum, he was cuffed, kicked and beaten. He dared not read his New Testament, fearing someone would throw it overboard; so he carried it in a hip pocket, wrapped in a piece of sailcloth. At night, he prayed for an opportunity to desert the ship, but was never permitted ashore at any of the small ports touched. Off the coast of German Southwest Africa one day, the ship foundered in a tropical hurricane, and Abraham, bruised, bleeding and unconscious, was washed ashore less than twenty miles from the town of Walvis Bay.

Sick, starving and in rags, he made his way to the town and was promptly arrested by authorities. Remaining in jail for seven weeks, he was then brought before a Captain Hein, who told him:

"I've arranged for you to ship as cabin boy on an English vessel that's now in port. In England, the captain will turn you over to proper officials who'll see that you're returned to your father. Report to the ship at dawn. It sails at noon. Don't miss it—we don't want Englishers in this country."

When I met Abraham in Ovampoland in 1911, he said:

"I'd rather have died than go back to my father. Father's name—Virginlow—had become symbolical of evil to me. One day in jail while reading my New Testament I'd determined to drop that name forever. I took the name 'Read,' Abe Read. Read had been my mother's maiden name."

And Abe Read lived to make his new name— through prayer—revered everywhere in Southwest and Portuguese West Africa. His prayer story is one of the first I obtained for my collection of answered prayer stories. I was eighteen then, and his story made such an impression on me that it's as strong today as when I first heard it.

We met in an Ovampo kraal, not far from the Caprivi

Strip on what is now the southeast border of Angola. I write this story from notes made then—forty-six years ago.

"I'd no sooner left Captain Hein's office," Read said, "than I took off northward. I was weak, forlorn and shoeless, but managed to keep going for about fourteen hours before collapsing under a thorn tree. I was so weak and shaky that I couldn't get my New Testament from my pocket. I thought I was dying and I asked God to let me live so that I might dedicate my life to Him. I was still praying when I fell asleep.

"I was awakened at dusk by someone shaking my shoulder, and looked up to see a middle-aged, brown-skinned native bending over me. I sat up, and the native —an Ovampo—pushed me gently down again. He handed me a leather pouch that had been tied around his waist, then said:

" 'Eat,' He pointed north. "That way you go.'

"I began to ask questions, but he shook his head and said:

" 'I make quick to go. Soldiers hunt me.' Then he trotted away into deepening shadows.

"The pouch contained about four double handfuls of uncooked corn meal, which I ate with tears of gratitude. For about a week, I traveled north, walking nights, hiding in daylight. I feared German patrols, but I never met one.

"One night I came to a lonely native hut, where I was fed a sort of stew, then told to head northeast and to keep traveling until I came to the village of a powerful Hottentot chieftain named Witboi who was in rebellion against the Germans.

"Fed and then directed along the way by friendly natives, I eventually arrived at Witboi's kraal. I wasn't permitted to meet him, but he sent word to me that I was welcome to live in a not-far-distant kraal of the Ovam-

po tribe for as long as I 'remained in peace.' " And
Abe Read remained in peace. He became a trader
among the Hottentots, Herero and Ovampo peoples,
and prospered moderately. He could have become
wealthy, but his stocks were given away freely during
the occasional years when hard times hit the kraals.
What Abe gave, however, was returned tenfold in the
natives' respect, trust and love.

From the first, he told the natives about Jesus and
about prayer. "I had no formal instruction in the
Bible," he told me, "so I didn't feel capable of teaching
religion. I merely translated the words printed in red in
the New Testament—Jesus' own words. Their message
was so clear and so simple that the natives readily understood them—and loved them.

"Witboi," Read continued, "maintained a sort of
guerrilla warfare with the Germans, and although I was
never involved in any way, the Germans made me pay
dearly. I had a big stock of skins and hides on hand that
I'd been commissioned to sell for the natives when a
German patrol—led by that same Captain Hein who'd
ordered me out of the country—arrived at the kraal.
Hein recognized me, confiscated all of my stock, including the skins and hides, and gave me three days in which
to get out of German territory—or else.

"I didn't feel that God wanted me to leave, for I'd
brought the teachings of Jesus to thousands. So I
walked to a lonely spot on the veldt to read my Bible
and to pray. The Bible and prayer were my only guidance. The Bible—particularly the New Testament—
pointed out my path, and prayer gave me courage and
strength to follow it.

"When I returned to the kraal, Hein and his men had
left. I spent the next few hours wondering how I'd be
able to pay the natives for their supplies which were in-

cluded in what I'd lost to Hein. Since the natives' supplies had been in my charge, I felt responsible.

"God answers prayer in wondrous ways! The next day just at sunset, a line of more than two hundred porters arrived from Witboi's kraal, each carrying between sixty and seventy pounds of hides on his head. A subchief with them said to me:

" 'Witboi says that you are not to leave. He sends these hides to replace the ones stolen. He says that you must now learn all of the Hottentot languages—fifteen —so that you can take God to all of his people.'

"I already spoke Hera and Kori, the two main Hottentot dialects, and believing that Witboi's dictate was God's answer to my prayer, I stayed on.

"The next year, Witboi entered into a truce with the Germans, and so for ten years I remained unmolested —trading constructively and teaching God's word.

"Then in 1904, the Germans broke off the truce, and Witboi's warriors took to the field again. Once more the Germans invaded the kraal. This time they set fire to my grass-thatched trading post, destroying everything, including one hundred and ten leopard skins that belonged to James McKinnie, an exceedingly wealthy man, and a great friend of Witboi's. I was in desperate straits, for McKinnie had already paid for the skins, and I had no cash with which to pay him back.

"Again God answered my prayers. Natives with whom I'd kept the faith for ten years now sent out hunters after cattle-destroying leopards. And only three days before McKinnie's wagons arrived to pick up his skins, those hunters brought exactly one hundred and ten skins to me as a gift.

"Once again I rebuilt my post, and with God's help survived through many vicissitudes. Then in 1908, the Germans dropped all opposition to Witboi's successors—Witboi died in 1905—and God has prospered me to this day."

In 1915, German Southwest Africa became a British protectorate, and Abe Read retired from trading to devote the last nine years of his life solely to the teaching of Christianity. In his will, Read left his mother's New Testament to James McKinnie, who in turn left it to John G. Lake, my missionary father.

So now you know why, when I hear the remark, "God and business don't mix," I invariably think of Abe Read.

WHILE CHECKING THE prayer story, "And So, He Peeled Potatoes," I talked with an old-time free-lance writer named Avery Smith, who said:

"Prayer got me my first break in the big-pay magazine field. From my home in Vancouver, B.C., I'd been bombarding slick paper editors with article ideas, hoping to get an assignment. Editors showed no enthusiasm, and I was pretty discouraged when one morning the mail brought a letter from a Collier's *editor telling me that if I'd go to Seattle and interview a man named Cato Fox, at the Fry Hotel, I'd get material for an article on which I could try my hand. The editor added: 'You'll have to do this article on speculation, but if we like it, we'll buy it.'*

"I was a string correspondent for the Vancouver World, *and my weekly earnings amounted to less than twenty-five dollars. Nevertheless, I'd managed to save close to fifty dollars—more than enough to get me to Seattle and back.*

"However, when I telephoned the provincial editor of the World, *he said that if I took time off, I'd be fired. I spent all that night worrying and sweating. Did I dare give up a job on the long chance that I'd be able to write an article satisfactory to* Collier's? *Since I couldn't make up my mind, I took the problem to a little old lady who'd encouraged me in my attempts to write. She said:*

"'It's a problem for prayer, Avery.' And we knelt right there and asked God's guidance. When we got up, she asked: 'Well?'

"'I go to Seattle,' I said.

"I went to the bank, took out my savings, put them in

58

my wallet and caught a train. I arrived in Seattle late Saturday afternoon, got a cheap room on First Avenue, went to a restaurant and ordered my meal, only to find before I'd taken a bite—that I'd lost my wallet.

"*After futilely searching my room and my suitcase, I went to the Fry Hotel and asked for Mr. Fox, and was told that he'd gone somewhere for the week end and wouldn't be back to the hotel until eight o'clock Monday morning.*

"*I ate no supper. The next day, Sunday, I stayed in my room, drinking glasses of water to assuage hunger pangs. That night I dreamed of food—platters of it—stacks of it—bowls of it. Monday morning as I walked to the Fry Hotel I was so hungry that the smell of breakfasts cooking in restaurants had me drooling.*

"*Promptly at eight o'clock, Mr. Fox entered the lobby. I showed him the letter from* Collier's. *In his room, he said:*

" '*I'm the nutrition director for a nationwide chain of drugstore restaurants.* Collier's *wants an article on the preparation of food for popular menus. The article has to be gustatorily exciting. Can you write about food?*'

" '*I'd rather write about food than anything else in the world,' I said.*

"*I roughed out the article right there in Fox's room. He read my first draft, and said:*

" '*Wonderful! Wonderful! You've captured everything—aroma, tang, titillation, gusto! Boy, you've given me an appetite! Let's go to breakfast.*'

"*After I'd downed bacon and eggs, toast, fried potatoes and three cups of coffee, I told Mr. Fox how I happened to be stuck in Seattle without money. He chuckled, handed me two twenty-dollar bills and said:*

" '*Add that to what* Collier's *pays you.*'

"Collier's *paid me seven hundred and fifty dollars.*"

And So, He Peeled Potatoes

SOMEWHERE IN THE UNITED STATES—EVEN AS YOU read this—a heavily laden truck with a supersecret engine is rolling along a highway. The engine is reported to be no larger than an ordinary brick. To test this engine, the truck has been climbing the steepest mountains, crossing the hottest, driest deserts, operating through rain, winds, sandstorms and blizzards for almost a year, twenty-four hours a day.

There are other engines, including several turbine engines, undergoing similar tests throughout the country, but these engines are in no way secret. Magazines have told all about them.

The truck with the mystery engine is driven by an acquaintance of mine, a one-time neighbor. His alternate driver is his brother. I'll call them Howard and Jerry Fifield—which are not their real names—for I was given this story with the understanding that until after the tests are completed, names are to be kept secret also.

Howard and Jerry Fifield are part Indian, although from appearance you'd never guess that. They got their unusual job through prayer—which is remarkable considering the fact that they were reared by Indians without the benefits of Christian teaching. Their mother had been religious, but following her death, when Howard was six, and Jerry four, their father—a wastrel—had disappeared, leaving the boys to the care of relatives. This is the way Howard told me their story:

"Jerry and I left home when I was sixteen, and hoboed our way across the country to Humboldt County,

California. We found work in a small lumber camp and settled down to a monotonous woods job. One day we found a broken-down truck engine that had been discarded as useless. We took it apart and since we decided we could fix it, we spent our savings for parts and eventually got the engine into running order. It seemed a great triumph to us, and we've lived and dreamed engines ever since. Eventually we became truck drivers.

"After many different driving jobs, we finally joined the ranks of redwood log haulers—the most expert truck drivers in the world. Redwood logs from the forests of northwestern California often weigh sixty thousand pounds, and are loaded on log trucks and driven to mills over narrow, winding mountain roads, roads that often hang on the edges of cliffs a thousand feet above the sea.

"Usually, the combined weight of the truck and logs is around seventy-three thousand pounds, and on steep climbs and downgrades, the load requires constant nursing by the driver. It's a terrible thing to see a tremendous load like that hurtling downhill with burned-out brakes, and it's not unusual in such cases for the driver to sacrifice his own life in order to save occupants of an oncoming car.

"Jerry and I ran logs from Crescent City to Eureka, California—one hundred miles. We loaded in the woods and unloaded at the mill, making two return trips each day—four hundred miles. In order to make two round trips a day, we often—when traveling empty on return trips—rolled at sixty-five miles an hour.

"If weather in northwestern California were always fair, such trips would be more or less matter-of-fact to capable drivers. But in the redwood area, fair days, particularly during winter, are few and far between. We usually bucked rain, fog, wind and sometimes even snow. The job took all we had—and we loved it.

"One day as I wheeled along a straight stretch running through the forest, I saw a truck pulled up beside the road. The driver had the hood up and seemed to be examining the engine. I pulled to a stop to see if I could help him. He was so intent that he didn't notice me until I got out of my cab and spoke. He looked up, startled, then slammed down the hood—but not before I'd caught a glimpse of an unbelievably small engine.

" 'No, thanks,' he said quickly, then climbed into his cab and took off at once—without gears!

"For days I could think of nothing but that tiny engine. I knew, of course, about turbine engines being tested throughout the country, but this engine was different; smaller, for one thing; smoother, if such a thing were possible. I asked questions of everyone—traffic officers, other drivers, millowners, tourists. I learned nothing except that the engine I'd seen was the invention of a Seattle, Washington, man.

"One day as my load was being weighed at a highway check station, a checker spoke about the mystery engine. "The driver of that truck said he was quitting his job as soon as his boss finds a driver to replace him,' he said.

"Naturally, from then on, I pictured myself driving that truck.

"Figuring it wouldn't be too hard to locate the inventor, I soon quit my job and went to Seattle. My hopes were high, but my luck was out, for although I combed that city—even its outlying districts—I couldn't get even a hint of who the inventor was, nor where he was.

"Came a day when my money ran out. Jerry wired me what he could, but it was only enough for another week or ten days, for Jerry had been laid off because of floods.

"I kept searching, but finally didn't have even bus fare back to California. Rain had been pouring for hours that day, and I was wet, weary and discouraged. My feet ached from pounding the pavement.

"I paused before a small neighborhood church, and on impulse I went into the vestibule and sat, dripping, on a bench. I was unlacing a boot when a voice said:

" 'Church is a good place to come when one is weary and troubled.'

"I looked up. The pastor stood just inside the open main doors.

" 'This is the first church I've ever come to,' I said.

"He looked kind, and said:

" 'You came to pray?'

" 'No, sir,' I said, 'I've done no praying since I was six.'

" 'Six?'

" 'My mother died when I was six. I remember she taught me some prayers, but after she died I was adopted by Indians.'

" 'Indians pray.'

" 'Not the ones I lived with.'

" 'But you know about God—He . . .'

" 'Well, I've lived in the redwoods a lot, and I don't think anyone can see those big trees without knowing God made them. Sometimes I've thought I'd like to know more about God, but—well, I've been pretty busy, and . . .'

"I didn't finish because the pastor didn't seem to be listening. I began to grow uncomfortable and moved to get to my feet. He said:

" 'Why are you here?'

" 'Well, sir, I—I don't really know. I just noticed the open doors, and . . . Well, I guess I'm pretty discouraged right now.'

" 'But you're a strapping, healthy young fellow!' he said. 'What's discouraged you so much?'

"His voice and his manner touched my heart. I began telling my story. I remember I finished by saying:

" 'And I've never wanted anything in my life like I want that particular job.'

"That pastor told me about God . . . and Jesus . . . and prayer. He made it seem so simple and natural that I never doubted the truth of his words. I asked many questions and received patient, kind answers. I've never forgotten some of the things he said. For instance:

" 'God is all good, my boy. Everything good comes from God, and we reach God through prayer. You love Good, therefore you love God. And because you love Him, His promises are for you. And remember, young fellow, He's promised you every good thing. However, *you're* not to judge what's good for you—God will do that.'

" 'Is that job I want good for me?' I asked.

" 'I don't see why not.'

" 'If I pray for it, will I get it?'

" 'I believe so—in God's own time—when He knows you're ready for it.'

" 'Will you help me pray for it?'

" 'Of course. Come on in.'

"We knelt and prayed side by side in that little church, and when we got up from our knees, I asked:

" 'What do I do now?'

" 'Have perfect trust. Take the first job offered you, work loyally at it—prayerfully—and be ready to move on when God opens the way. If your heart's desire seems long in coming, pray for patience and for faith. And pray always with love. Good-by now, Fifield—and God go with you.'

"It was still raining as I left the church, but the world seemed brighter and more beautiful. I put in my pocket the red-letter testament that the pastor had given me, and walked along Second Avenue. At the corner of

Union, I bought the evening papers and turned to the want ads. There were no jobs I could handle, and as I turned up Union I jingled the few coins in my pocket. Something had to happen—soon.

"After a few blocks I paused to look in a restaurant window, and realized I was hungry. I counted my money—ninety-six cents. This was a high-priced res-taurant; I'd better find a cheaper one. I was turning away when I saw a small cardboard sign propped against a cake tray in a corner of the window.

POTATO PEELER WANTED

"I walked back towards First Avenue where I knew I could get three whopping hot cakes for a quarter. I'd walked nearly one block when I got the shocking thought that that potato peeling job was the first to cross my horizon since I'd prayed. It wasn't a pleasant thought. I told myself I wasn't supposed to take a me-nial job like that. I took a few hesitant steps, paused, then turned back, saying to myself: 'You've gotta obey the rules, guy. You can't play it both ways.'

"It wasn't easy for me to enter that restaurant, but I did. I pushed aside a curtain in the window, took out the sign and handed it to the man standing beside the cash register. He was the proprietor, a pleasant-voiced Greek.

" 'You don't look like a bum,' he said.

" 'I'm not.'

" 'A drunk?'

" 'No.'

" 'Well,' he shrugged, 'it's none of my business why you want this kind of a job.' He led me to the basement, showed me two washtubs filled with potatoes, handed me a paring knife and said:

" 'Peel 'em thin, please,' then went upstairs.

"After pulling up a full sack of potatoes for a seat, I began work. At first the peelings were wastefully thick, but six hours after I'd started, when the second tubful was finished, I was doing a good job. I put on my coat, went upstairs and the proprietor handed me four dollars and fifty cents—seventy-five cents an hour—then led me to a back booth, handed me a menu and said:

" 'Order a good meal.'

"After work on the second day, I went after a truck-driving job I'd heard was available, but learned that only union drivers could work in the Seattle area. After several other futile attempts to get work through help-wanted ads, I stopped fussing, bought a patented potato peeler in a dime store and made a game of cutting down the time it took to peel two tubs of potatoes. I finally was able to do it in three hours, but the Greek paid me for six hours anyway.

"With time to spare, I began studying the New Testament, and following the pastor's advice, I concentrated on the passages printed in red—Jesus' own words.

"One afternoon the proprietor walked back to the booth where I always ate and found me reading my testament.

" 'I sure would like to know your story, mister,' he said. 'What are you doing—peeling potatoes in a restaurant?'

"Well, as I've said, that Greek was a nice fellow, so I told him how I'd hunted in vain for the inventor of the marvelous mystery engine, hoping to get the job of driving it; told him how I'd learned to pray; how it had happened that I'd taken his peeling job. He seemed satisfied, but only moderately interested.

"A few days later, the proprietor came downstairs with a middle-aged, gray-haired man who said to me:

" 'Nick here, has told me your story, but if you don't object, I'd like to hear it again, from you.'

" 'Look, mister,' I said, "I'm just a guy who's sawing wood until a job I'm after materializes. My story concerns only myself.'

" 'Tell it to me anyhow,' he said.

"So a bit resentfully, I told it. When I'd finished, he asked:

" 'How long will you stick at this job if the other one doesn't open up?'

" 'I don't know.' I said. 'All I know is that I'm following that pastor's advice, and trying to let God direct me. And I still believe I'll find that inventor.'

" 'You think he'd give you the job?'

" 'Why not? There's no better truck driver or engine man than I am, and I was told that's the sort of man he wants.'

" 'Quite true,' he said. 'Nick and I've been friends a long while. He's been watching you, Fifield. Nick thinks you're the very man I need.'

"I got to my feet, felt weak kneed, then sat down again. "You're the inventor,' I said.

" 'Yes. Finish out your day here and come see me tomorrow.' He handed me his card.

"There you have it," Howard Fifield told me. "I got the job, sent for Jerry, and we've been pushing that truck around ever since. And both Jerry and I thank God every day for the simple but important lesson we've learned—to pray in faith, then await God's time for the answer."

JEAN LOUIS AGASSIZ, naturalist, geologist and professor of zoology at Harvard University from 1848 until his death in 1873, was the ablest teacher of science that America has ever had. So skillful was he that every notable teacher of natural history in the United States for the second half of the nineteenth century was at some time, a pupil of his, or of one of his students.

At a period when many self-styled intellectuals thought it smart to be atheists, Agassiz taught that each species of plant and animal life was "a thought of God," and that their fundamental unities were "associations of ideas in the Divine Mind."

Agassiz was tall, solidly built, with a noble head and a warm smile. Of his warmth, the people of Cambridge said that one had less need of an overcoat in passing Agassiz' house than any other in the city.

This extraordinary teacher and his students began each class with prayer. John Greenleaf Whittier was so impressed to see Agassiz "bow his mighty mind in the presence of nature, and the God from whence all nature comes" that he described the scene thus:

Said the master to the youth:
'We have come in search of truth,
Trying with uncertain key
Door by door of mystery;
We are searching through His laws,
To the garment-hem of cause,
Him, the endless, unbegun,
The Unnameable, the One,

Light of all our light the source
Life of life and force of force.

By past efforts unavailing
Doubt and error, loss and failing,
Of our weakness made aware,
On the threshold of our task
Let us light and guidance ask,
Let us pause in silent prayer!'

Then the master in his place,
Bowed his head a little space,
And the leaves, by soft air stirred,
Lapse of wave and cry of bird,
Left the solemn hush unbroken
Of that wordless prayer unspoken,
While its wish, on earth unsaid,
Rose to heaven interpreted.

He Found God in an Umbrella

THERE ARE HUNDREDS OF CASES ON RECORD OF MEN and women who turned to God while inmates of German prison camps, but on young Albert Flamin, Flemish farmer, the mental and physical torment to which he'd been subjected had the opposite effect—he became bitterly atheistic. Peace brought him release from prison, but only increased his suffering and bitterness. Finally, when pain, poverty and loneliness were no longer bearable, Albert went to his knees crying that unless he could find God, he was lost. He asked for a revela-

tion—and God gave it him—through a hole in an umbrella.

Here is Albert's astonishing story, told to me by Albert through an interpreter, Professor Pierre Jouan, for-
merly of Brussels University.

Albert Flamin, twenty-one, and Maria Vlonts, eighteen, were married in East Flanders on May 17, 1940.
As they stepped from the little one-room church following the ceremony, they paused hand-in-hand to delight
in the first warm sunshine after weeks of fog and rain.
Noises of a summer day were all about—the twittering
of birds, grasshoppers buzzing, rustlings in the grass,
the far-off creaking of a cart wheel, the bawling of a distant cow. And there was another sound that echoed
from the mountainous cumulus clouds high overhead—
the muted thunder of German bombers. Albert, who
had just finished his year of military service, thought
they were Belgian.

Weeds and hedges that lined the narrow dirt road
were still clean and fresh from recent rains, and Albert,
Maria and the four families who had attended the wedding sang as they trudged the three miles to the tiny
hamlet that was the home of all of them, and the roar of
the bombers diminished and died.

The hamlet, too small to have a name, consisted of
five identical three-room, white-washed, dirt-walled,
thatched cottages surrounding a central pond. Back of
each cottage was a pen for chickens, and one for the
family pig, but seldom were pigs or chickens found in
their pens. They, like the ducks, lived a sort of commu-
nal life on the shores of the pond.

One of the cottages belonged to Albert, and he had
lived there alone since his parents had died when he was
fourteen. He had cared for the domestic animals and
worked the three acres as efficiently and industriously
as if he had been a man. At twenty, when drafted into

the Army, he was as prosperous as any of his neighbors. Shortly before his discharge, he met Maria and they had fallen in love.

Beside the pond, the neighbors dispersed to their own homes, leaving the young couple to themselves. Maria spent most of that afternoon admiring the two half-grown black pigs, the twelve chickens, the ragged rooster, the listless hairy dog that Albert had trained to haul a cart, and the six ducks that spent their time waddling between the cottage and the pond. An orphan, Maria never dreamed she would ever have so many possessions, and she was filled with gratitude to God for having blessed her so abundantly. As she knelt beside the bed to say her prayers that night, she waited for Albert to join her. When he didn't, she said:

"We must thank God for His goodness, Albert."

"My father taught me that there is no God," Albert said.

"But Albert . . ."

"Our neighbors pray to God, and they have prosperity. I have never prayed, and I, too, have prosperity."

"But Albert, there *is* a God!"

"I do not deny it, Maria. It's just that I don't think it matters. Those of our neightbors who do *not* believe in God enjoy all the good things that the others do, who *do* believe. Father said that God does not exist—and he was even more prosperous than most small farmers."

"But was your father happy? Was his heart at peace?"

"He was bitter about the terrible things that were done to him and to others during World War I."

"In the orphanage," Maria said, "I was taught that all good things come from God. You have many good things, Albert—this little farm, your health, the animals, this house to live in. It's easy to forget God when everything goes all right, Albert, but I wonder if you won't feel the need of Him if things were to go wrong?"

Albert laughed and kissed her. "What could go wrong?" he asked.

He was soon to know.

During the night they were awakened by rumbling detonations of distant bombs. Maria was frightened, but snuggled back to sleep when Albert assured her that the Belgian army was probably holding simulated war maneuvers.

They were up at dawn, fed the pigs, ducks and chickens, warmed the soup left from last night's meal for their breakfast, and were gathering hoes, rakes and shovels to be used in their work in the fields, when six tarp-covered trucks roared up the road, turned into their yard and braked to shrieking stops. Gray-clad, steel-helmeted soldiers debouched from the trucks, and holding bayoneted rifles across their bodies, rushed every house in the hamlet. Albert was tossed into one truck and Maria into another.

And so it was that Albert learned that Germany's invasion of Belgium had begun seven days before his capture.

Five years and one month later, racked with rheumatism, his weight down from one hundred and eighty-five to one hundred and nineteen pounds, Albert was released from prison camp by Allied troops, shipped to Brussels, where he was outfitted with two pairs of worn army shoes, a used army uniform, given a handful of small silver coins and ordered to return to his hamlet and begin farming again. He was so sure that Maria was dead that he didn't bother to make inquiries concerning her.

To save his few silver coins, he walked the ninety miles to his farm. He found the fields torn by shellfire, the cottages burned, the pond filled with junked military equipment. For an hour, he sat brooding among the litter of his old home, then began the long, painful walk back to Brussels.

Authorities refused him aid because he'd disobeyed their orders to stay on his farm. That there was no farm left was not accepted as a legitimate excuse, so Albert began a wearisome search for work. For more than two weeks he dragged himself about the city begging for a job—any sort of job. He slept in alleys, under bridges, in tumbled-down sheds. He ate what he could scavenge. Then finally, at the Flower Market in the Grande Place, he was put to work doing odd jobs and running errands. He was paid in tips, which were seldom more than enough to pay rent on a slum room. Able to buy only meager supplies of food, he was soon in a state of semistarvation.

During the next six months or so, Albert was in constant pain as he went about his errands. One morning as he sat on a curb too ill to walk another step, a passing physician stopped to examine him briefly, then asked him what he ate.

"Potatoes and bread," Albert said, and added: "and sometimes soup from the potato peelings."

"But my dear fellow," the doctor said, "you must have soup with green vegetables and plenty of meat in it. Your painful joints are caused by poor diet. You must eat better. Eat well, my man, and you'll get well."

"Thank you," Albert said, and thinking of the few pennies that must last another week, he laughed in the doctor's face.

Finally one day while he lay in his chilly room too sick to work, his landlady brought him a bowl of hot cabbage soup, then wrapped him in a bedquilt to, as she said, "make you sweat to break your fever." Albert, semidelirious, kept calling the woman "Maria." Later, when he was convalescing, the landlady, who'd brought more soup, asked:

"Who is Maria, Monsieur Flamin?"

"Maria was my wife," Albert said. "The Germans took her, and she died."

"Many died," the landlady said, "but not all who were imprisoned. I know a Maria who didn't die, although she was made to suffer much. She, too, works at the Flower Market, and like you, is very lonely, for her man died in the war. Someday perhaps you will meet her. And who knows, you may comfort each other."

"Yes," Albert said, "I am lonely, but for my own Maria. Many times I have wished to be dead."

"Is it so, poor man? Well, there were times during the war when I too, wished to die. But the good God helped me to bear my sorrows. This Maria, monsieur, who is also lonely, works for Madam Cosson in the big flower stall opposite Hôtel de Ville. When you are able to be around again, you should look her up. No?"

"No," Albert said.

Late on Christmas Eve, several weeks later, Albert was sent to pick up two potted azaleas at Madam Cosson's flower stall. Madam Cosson, busy with customers, called to a young woman who was making up corsages at a back counter to "bring those azaleas in the lavender-wrapped pots." Carrying a flowering plant in each hand, the woman came toward Albert, recognized him, gasped, and dropped the pots with a crash.

The next moment Albert held his own Maria in his arms.

When the couple finally made Madam Cosson understand what had happened, she burst into tears, took Albert to her massive bosom and hugged him until he gasped. Then she shooed her bewildered customers from the stall, closed up shop, told Albert and Maria to wait, and rushed into the night. She returned with a tin of chocolate and some little Christmas cakes, pushed them into Albert's hands, and again broke into tears as she watched the seemingly dazed couple walk away into the darkness.

Albert and Maria had been in his room only a few minutes when the landlady came in with a large cup of hot soup. She listened openmouthed as Albert told how he'd found his Maria, then, like Madam Cosson, wept hugged Albert, kissed Maria and cried:

"It is of the good God—the dear, good God! How happy we are! We must have more soup!" She thumped down the stairs, to return beaming with a second steaming cup.

Too exhausted physically and emotionally to eat, Albert and Maria lay down side by side on his pallet on the floor. Almost instantly, they were asleep, their fingers clinging.

For the next two weeks, Albert and Maria were like children living a happy fairy tale. Each morning Albert escorted Maria to Madam Cosson's, then spent the day going from flower stall to flower stall seeking what odd jobs he could get. When the day's work was done, he and Maria would walk home in the darkness—holding hands.

Maria knelt briefly each morning and night to thank God for His blessings, but Albert refused to pray with her "because," he told her, "it is plain to me that there is no God."

"Albert! How can you say such a thing after the way God brought us together again! He has been good to us, Albert, He . . ."

"Good!" Albert interrupted. "Would a good God permit wars? Would a good God permit starvation and horror and torture? I tell you, Maria, I've seen terrible things."

"Yes, Albert—terrible things. I, too, have seen them.

And for a time during those first awful days, I thought that God had deserted His world. But I saw starving men give their last morsels of food to hungry children. I saw men and women accept punishment so that others might be spared it. There were seven thousand prisoners in the first camp to which I was sent, Albert, and I believe that *every one of them* would gladly have given his life to save his fellows. Among those prisoners I saw greatness of heart beyond anything I could have believed. Men, women—even children—became godlike in their willingness to sacrifice themselves for others, even unto death. As I witnessed these things, I always thought of the words of Jesus at the Last Supper:

> *Greater love hath no man than this, that a man lay down his life for his friends.*

"And it was shown to me, Albert, that the war was caused by only a few evil men—that the *peoples* of the world themselves are basically good, and that this goodness, which is also love, burst forth like blooming flowers even in pits of horror. Such self-sacrifice, such love for those who suffer—that is of God. It *is* God."

"But why, if God is good, must there be wars?"

"I asked that question of an old, old man who remained kindly and helpful to his very last moment. He answered me by saying:

" 'It may be that man has fallen into a dark pit so that he can better see the stars.' "

"Stars," Albert said. "You know, Maria, I've hardly ever seen the stars. On the farm, I went to bed at dusk so that I could arise at dawn to do my work. What did the old man mean, 'see the stars'?"

"I think he meant that in times of security and peace, man becomes too busy with his affairs to think of God, that from the pitlike darkness of suffering, we look upward because there's no other direction in which to look."

"But Maria," Albert said, "How about us? Why should we suffer—we who have never harmed anyone? Why should everything we have be taken from us—our farm, our cottage, all we ever had?"

"All, Albert?"

"What have we left?"

"We have life, Albert, and love for each other—for humanity. To love truly, Albert, is to know God—for God is Love. God is all good things. And Albert, we have faith. And having faith, all things that are good for us will be ours."

"You mean we'll have health again? The farm? The cottage beside the pond? No more hunger and cold?"

"Prayer works, Albert. I *know*. And, *mon cher,* the time has come for us to pray together, for whether you realize it of not, Albert, you *do* believe in God."

"Do I?"

"Yes—for you're a good man, Albert. Goodness is of God. And you have seen God, Albert. You've seen Him in the growing things you love so much—the plants, the wild flowers in your fields, the two rivers that run to the sea near the cottage—in the reflection of the sun on your pond, in the seasons for planting and harvesting, in the wind that brought rain to your crops, in the moon and in the stars—in my love for you, and your love for me. Kneel with me, Albert, and we'll ask God to become very *real* to you. We'll thank Him for having enabled you to live in such a way that you can respect yourself, for respect for one's self is the first step toward loving God."

"But Maria," Albert said, "I've always thought that God is not. You're causing me to think new thoughts. If a man has not learned to have faith, how can he pray?"

"Such a one must pray for faith," Maria said. "Kneel with me, Albert."

They knelt, and Maria prayed. When they arose, Albert said:

"What do I do now that we've prayed?"

"From now on you do nothing of yourself, Albert. You do what God wants you to. You must trust Him to direct you—you must know that He loves you—that you love Him."

"All this is easy to say," Albert said, "but how can I *know* that God is directing me? How can I know that the thoughts I think are His, and not mine?"

"Because you'll think only good thoughts. You'll deny entrance to your heart of such evil thoughts as worry, fear, anger, anxiety and hatred. Good thoughts are God's thoughts. If the thing that you would do *feels* good to you—if it is something that will not cause you to dislike yourself—then, Albert, you may act with confidence and faith."

"You did not talk this way in the old days, Maria. Where have you learned such things?"

"It's that I have read much in the New Testament, and have prayed often that God enable me to understand what I read. We shall read God's Word together."

"But you know that I cannot read, Maria."

Maria laughed. "Such a one for difficulties!" she said. "It makes no problem that *you* cannot read, *mon infant,* for *I* shall read to *you.*"

During the next three weeks, Albert's budding faith was severely tried. Hardly had he and Maria risen from their knees when heavy rains began, and the weather turned cold. Albert got wet, and his rheumatism flared so that he couldn't work. Then unexpectedly, Madam Cosson sold her business, and the new proprietor let Maria go. She promptly took over Albert's odd jobs, in order to be able to buy inexpensive foods and pay the rent when it fell due. Albert fumed and fussed and fretted until one evening Maria arrived home unusually weary, flopped on a chair and said:

"Can you like yourself as a complainer, Albert?"

"I hate myself," he said, "lying here creaky and cranky and useless while you do all the work. It seems strange to me that praying seems only to have increased our troubles."

"Do you know more than God?"

"That is a foolish question."

"We asked God to direct us, no?"

"Well?"

"Would you tell God how He should go about helping us?"

"But Maria, the rains . . . no job . . ."

"We must believe, Albert, that what is happening now is part of God's plan for us. If our way seems dark, we must believe that it leads to sunlight. It may be that God wants us to do other things. We need not try to understand—we need only to pray that our faith keeps burning brightly. I see you've kept the soup hot. That is good. Now, together, we will thank God for the soup."

"Your faith makes mine stronger," Albert said. "I will think good thoughts, Maria. To me, the way of faith is strange. I will try to be more like you, my good one."

A few days later, while the rain was pouring down, Maria's employer thrust an old umbrella into her hand and sent her to deliver a package. As she passed Hôtel de Ville, a well-dressed Englishman burst from a doorway, took the umbrella from her, thrust some coins into her hand and said hastily:

"Buy another umbrella, woman. I need this one."

Too astonished to protest, Maria watched him hurry down the street, then counted the coins he'd given her.

There were enough to buy two umbrellas. She delivered the package, hurried back to her employer and paid him what he asked for the umbrella he'd lent her. Then she walked to the place of business of an umbrella maker, bought one at wholesale and sold it at good profit to a dripping pedestrian. She bought two more umbrellas, sales netted her more than a whole week's pay at Madam Cosson's.

Delighted with the success of her first venture into business, Maria—wet, bedraggled, her feet squelching in her shoes—stopped at a market on her way home and bought a large, round loaf of bread, cabbage, turnip tops, barley, carrots and a marrow bone. She told Albert about the umbrella sales as she prepared the first truly rich soup they'd had in weeks. Albert grew thoughtful as they ate, and finally said:

"You have brought news of the best, *ma chere,* but when the rains stop—what them?"

"I have thought of that problem, too," Maria said, breaking more bread into her soup, "and it is solved. When the sun shines, and none will buy umbrellas, I will stay home with you and manufacture umbrellas— for today I learned where to buy the materials. We will sell, during wet weather, the umbrellas we make in good weather. Thus, we become prosperous and grow fat. Is not that a beautiful thought, my thin one?"

Came the first of several days of gusty, showery weather, and Maria returned from shopping with handles, ferrules, stems, ribs and black cotton cloth for two umbrellas. She also brought special pliers, a tack hammer, scissors, needles and thread. Excitedly they started assembling their first two umbrellas, but by the time they were finished, Albert's finger joints had become swollen and painful.

Albert's pain became constant, and sleep became almost impossible—for the slightest movement sent agony shooting into his elbows, shoulders and neck. Maria finally called a doctor who told Albert that while his illness stemmed from improper diet, it was being aggravated by deep-seated feelings of frustration, fear and anxiety. Albert denied having such emotions, but was told that he probably wasn't aware of them because they were buried in his subconscious.

"But I've willed all such thoughts out of my mind," Albert protested.

"My dear man," the doctor said, "I've been practicing medicine for thirty years, and I've never yet seen the person who can *will* the feelings of guilt, fear and hostility from his nature. Nor do I believe it can be done—at least, not permanently—by psychoanalysis. But there *is* one simple, certain way to rid yourself forever of destructive emotions, and that's by prayer—true prayer."

"But I *have* prayed, sir," Albert said.

"Well, then," said the doctor, "you prayed from your head. God answers only true prayers—that come from the heart." He turned to Maria, felt her pulse, lifted an eyelid, took out a stethoscope and listened to her chest, then turned to Albert and said:

"Your wife, too, is suffering from improper diet. For both of you, I prescribe eggs, cereals, milk, occasional meat—and frequent prayer."

When the doctor had gone, Maria said cheerfully:

"Well, *mon cher*, to buy such foods, one must sell umbrellas." She put on her threadbare coat, took the two finished umbrellas, and said: "It's threatening rain again, Albert, and in the streets will be some who fear to get wet. When I've sold these two I shall return with the foods demanded by the good doctor."

For some time after Maria had gone out, Albert lay on his pallet with despair smothering him like a blanket. If his cure and Maria's health depended on costly foods, their case was hopeless, for street sales of umbrellas would never be enough. Now that the doctor had called his attention to Maria's health, he realized she'd been growing thinner, more easily wearied. She was overworked and underfed. His own Maria! Weak, ill, in pain and hopelessly frustrated, he was unable to keep the tears from his eyes. Then, suddenly forgetting pain, he got to his knees, lifted his face to the skies and cried: "God, dear God, why have You permitted me to become lost—lost? I have prayed for faith, and You have not answered. Now, God, I pray again—this time not for myself, but for my Maria. It is not right, God, that You should permit my lack of faith to injure my Maria, for You, God, You know she is good—good—good."

This time, Albert had put his whole troubled heart into his prayer, and when it was finished he slumped forward on his face and lay drained of emotion. Gradually, a sense of peace descended on him and he slept— to awaken abruptly. In a sort of frenzy, he got up and began assembling an umbrella. He'd finished it and was testing it by opening and closing it when he noticed there was a half inch tear in the cloth about fifteen inches below the ferrule.

Deciding that a patch was called for, Albert took the scissors and cut the rent into a neat, round hole about the size of a finger ring; then, suddenly realizing that Maria could have made a much neater repair by careful mending of the original small tear, he muttered in annoyance, closed the umbrella and stood it in a corner. He noticed that sunshine had dispersed the threat of rain, and acting on impulse, he went into the hall, mounted a ladder to the roof, stripped off his shirt and lay down. Soothed by the sun's warmth, he soon fell asleep.

Maria, returning home shortly after, placed her groceries on the table, saw Albert's tools, looked around and saw the newly made umbrella in the corner, then busied herself while waiting for Albert to show up. Half an hour later, when he still hadn't made an appearance, she went looking for him, and finally located him on the roof—still asleep. Fearing he would sunburn, but not wishing to waken him, she brought the umbrella from the corner of their room, opened and placed it over Albert so that it shaded him. She sat beside him, listening to his deep, steady breathing, and thanking God silently that the lines of pain were erased from Albert's face.

Dusk fell, then darkness. The sun retired beyond the western sea, but the night grew sultry, seeming hotter than the day had been. Stars shone with unusual brilliance, and a storm was brewing. Tomorrow it would rain, but not tonight. Albert slept comfortably on, with nothing under him but the roof. After all, he had slept on bare concrete floors, winter and summer, for five years. Maria decided to let him sleep, and with a brief prayer for his welfare, went to her pallet downstairs.

I think it best to let Albert tell the rest of his story himself.

"I awakened near midnight," he said, "free of pain, and so comfortable—so rested—that I didn't even try to understand why I was in unfamiliar surroundings. I turned on my back, noted the umbrella over me, wondered idly how it had got there, and stared with mild interest at a bright star that shone through a hole in the umbrella cloth. Soon I got the feeling that the star was an eye staring back at me. I became fascinated.

"Then the star disappeared beyond the edge of the hole. Thinking I had moved and lost sight of it, I shifted my head until I sighted it through the hole again. I lay unmoving—watching—and this time the star passed from sight again within a few minutes. It seemed to me that the star had moved—and I felt a thrill of fear, for I *knew* that stars didn't move. Again I sighted it through the hole. I remained absolutely unmoving, and again, the star moved out of my vision. I sat up dismayed. The star *was* moving!

"In a sort of mild panic, I pushed the umbrella aside and stared upward into the star fields, concentrating on three stars almost directly overhead. Soon a strange thing happened; I seemed to be slowly—slowly—slowly drifting toward the east. I'd discovered the turning of the earth!

"You must understand," Flamin said, "that I'd stayed in school only long enough to learn the alphabet and numbers. Oddly, although I hadn't learned to read, I was good with figures. In fact, I know now that mathematics was an unusual talent of mine. Anyhow, until that night of discovery, I'd thought of the stars as being fixed overhead in a flat plane—points of light about the size of candle flames. I'd never asked myself how they'd gotten there. They were just there, as were trees and the mountains.

"From the three stars, which I now know to be Orion's Belt, I shifted my gaze to the Big Dipper, which my father had once pointed out to me, along with the North Star. Incidentally, I learned later that the star I'd first seen through the hole in the umbrella was Merak, the middle star of the Dipper's handle.

"As I watched the Dipper, I lost the sensation of the earth's turning. Instead, I grew puzzled, for the Dipper, which had been above the North Star when I'd first seen it, seemed to have wheeled an eighth of a circle. I must have dozed off then, for when I awakened, dawn was shimmering on the horizon, and the fading Dipper was directly west of the North Star.

"Nothing that ever happened to me had so fascinated me as these strange movements of the stars. All that day, I fidgeted with impatience because the night seemed so long in coming. In the afternoon, rain came, with thunder and lightning, but the weather cleared at sunset, and I was able to spend another night observing the bright worlds overhead—which I'd never really seen before.

"That night, I learned to recognize—without knowing their names—the constellations Cepheus, Cassiopeia, Perseus, Draco and a couple of others. I also figured that these constellations revolved about the North Star. I was like a man in a dream, literally dazed with wonder and awe. And I knew I could never rest from studying the stars until I knew all there was to learn about them.

"When the thought came to me that I could view the stars only on clear nights, I was inspired to create a sky of my own.

"That first night on the roof, while looking at Merak through the hole in the umbrella, I'd seen faint images of the brighter stars through the surrounding cloth. Excited with an idea I now know was inspired by prayer, I took the umbrella with the hole in it to the roof one evening, arranged it on some empty boxes so that the ferrule pointed to the North Star, the handle pointed south and the lower rim of the umbrella coincided with the northern horizon. Then looking up through the fabric, I marked on it, with chalk, the positions of all of the stars I could see. It was a simple matter then to insert, in their proper places, the stars in the constellations whose light did not penetrate the cloth. Downstairs, I borrowed a tin of white paint from the landlady and, using a small brush, I carefully painted the chalked-in stars. Next morning when the paint was dry, I closed the umbrella, wound it neatly, fastened the binding strap and put the umbrella in the tiny room closet.

"Shortly after noon that day it began to rain, so Maria and I each hurried into the street with two umbrellas to sell—for money was needed again for the expensive vegetables and meat Maria was using to make the nourishing soups that were helping to cure my swollen, painful joints. The other part of the cure, we believed, was because prayer had now eliminated much of the wartime bitterness from my heart. Maria suggested I try making sales in the vicinity of the town hall, while she worked among the crowds in the market place.

"I tucked my two umbrellas under an arm, pulled my coat collar up around my neck and splashed my way along the street. Near Maison du Roi, I offered a bearded man an umbrella. He hesitated, then accepted it, opened it, held it over his head and fumbled in a pocket for money. Suddenly a stream of water from a hole in the umbrella ran down the back of his neck. He looked upward in annoyance, started to say something, but instead, stood staring at the constellations painted up there among the ribs.

"I opened the other umbrella, held it toward him, and grasping the leaking one by the handle, tried to exchange them. He brushed me aside and stood in the downpour, aiming the umbrella toward the north and revolving it slowly while muttering:

" 'Remarkable! So simple! Remarkable!'

" 'I'm sorry, sir,' I said, 'that umbrella got mixed with the ones I have for sale. You're getting wet, sir.'

"He looked at me curiously. 'Why have you painted constellations in this umbrella?' he asked. 'They're quite accurately placed, I see. Are you a student of astronomy?'

" 'I'm not sure I know what astronomy is,' I said, 'but I painted the stars in there because I thought perhaps I could study them this way when the weather's too bad to . . .'

"He grasped my arm and pulled me into the shelter of a small portico. 'There's a story here,' he said, 'that I must know more about. I'm Professor Jouan, an instructor of astronomy at Brussels University. Now, my man, begin at the beginning.'

"His eyes were so kind and his voice so friendly that I opened my heart—told him everything that had happened since the German Invasion. When I'd finished, he said:

" 'So you prayed. That is as it should be. And I think, my dear boy, that these constellations in the umbrella are not only an answer to *your* prayers, but to *mine* too. You see, since the war many college students are pitifully poor, but even the poorest must use an umbrella on occasion. Therefore, having purchased an umbrella that is also a star map, students can study sidereal rotations day or night—for this umbrella, rotated properly, can portray star movements almost as accurately as the stars themselves. Furthermore, this umbrella can be made to indicate the positions of the stars thereon for any minute, any hour and any day of the year. Where do you live?'

"I gave him our address, and said: 'But it is not a place to which a man such as you would care to visit. Slums . . .'

" 'I will talk to my students,' he said, 'and it may be that when I come to visit you tomorrow night, I'll bring orders for twenty—thirty—maybe fifty umbrellas. Is that good news?'

"My heart was so full that I could only nod my head.

"Professor Jouan arrived the next night just as Maria and I were finishing our soup. He entered with five or six books in his arms, started to greet us, but stood still, sniffing.

" 'Ha!' he said. 'Such an aroma of good soup. I must have a bowl of it—maybe two bowls. I am weary of sipping dishwater at my place of boarding.' He put the books on a chair, placed his hat upon them, sat in another chair, put his hands on his spread knees and said: 'Now, madam, the soup, please.'

"He took the bowl Maria handed him in both hands, crooked a finger about the handle of the wooden spoon to keep it from poking him in the eye, lifted the bowl to his lips and sipped noisily. When the bowl was half empty, he said to Maria:

" 'I drink such soup with gusto, madam, because of its excellence. A little more cabbage, perhaps . . .' He drank the rest of the liquid, spooned up the vegetables, wiped his beard with a handkerchief, handed the empty bowl to Maria and said:

" 'Your husband, madam, has brought the Heavens into an umbrella. Not many of my pupils have such an interest in the stars as he—therefore, I have conceived the idea of making your husband my pupil also. To that end, I have brought him these books—written by men greatly versed in astronomy. He will study them well. No?'

" 'I never learned to read,' I said. 'My wife reads to me.'

"For a moment, he seemed perturbed, then his white teeth flashed in a smile, and he said:

" 'Then, we must start to learn. The good wife will teach you, and, my friend, the lessons start tonight. Is this not so, madam?'

" 'It is so, monsieur,' Maria said.

" 'And now,' Professor Jouan went on, 'I instruct you to remove the star cover from the umbrella and spread it upon new cloth, as a pattern. Paint in the constellations exactly, and proceed to make me thirty-eight umbrellas of excellent workmanship.'

"While Maria and I stood speechless at our good fortune, Professor Jouan took a worn billfold from his coat pocket, removed a small sheaf of money and placed it on the table, saying:

" 'This is one half the money that I will owe you. It is to buy the materials, and also to buy more vegetables so that I can enjoy another such soup when I return. The balance of the money will be yours when you have finished all the umbrellas. Is this good news?'

" 'God bless you, monsieur,' Maria said, and started to cry.

" 'Such tears are a medicine,' the professor said, patting my shoulder. 'I go now, but will return. Remain with God.'

"I, too, had tears as I watched him close the door behind him.

"When I turned to Maria, she was on her knees. I knelt beside her, and together we thanked God for having lifted so much of our burden from us. That night, Maria began teaching me the alphabet.

"Two weeks later, when Professor Jouan returned, our little factory had completed twenty-two of the umbrellas. He examined them, praised the workmanship, and said:

" 'Tonight, Albert, I will begin to teach you about the stars. As you probably know, the stars do not move around the earth—it is the earth that moves, so that the stars seem to rise in the east and set in the west. Do you understand this?'

" 'This has been told to me,' I said, 'and also that the earth is round like a ball.'

" 'Yes,' the professor said, 'a great ball—a sphere that is twenty-five thousand miles around. That is large, is it not?'

" 'Very large,' I said.

" 'You have seen the sun?'

" 'But, of course.'

" 'Do you know what a *million* is?'

" 'Yes. I am not ignorant of numbers.'

" 'The sun, Albert, is one million, three hundred and

eighty thousand times larger than the earth! The sun seems small only because it is far away.'

" 'I believe,' I said.

" 'The stars that you see in the sky are suns, Albert. There are *billions* upon *billions* of them. Not *millions,* Albert, but *billions*. Many of those *billions* of suns are many times larger than our sun. One such sun is called Rigel. That is the star of which you told me when you described the constellation Orion—the one you watched that first night on the roof. Remember? Well, Rigel is far, far away, yet he is a mere step from us compared with the distances from us of untold *billions* of other stars! You have seen the Milky Way?'

" 'Yes, sir.'

" 'Well, my boy, our sun, our earth, and the other planets of our solar system are part of the Milky Way. And the Milky Way contains more than forty *billion* other suns. Among that vast concourse of suns, our sun is one of the smallest.'

"Maria and I sat spellbound as the professor unfolded some of the marvels of Creation. As I began to understand a little of the magnificence and grandeur of God's universe, I could actually feel my pettiness, bitterness, querulousness and cynicism being dissolved by a surging faith. The professor looked at his watch and said:

" 'The night is fine, and the moon has not yet risen to dim the stars. Let us go to the roof, where I hope to be able to show you another marvel.'

"On the roof, we waited a few minutes until our eyes had adjusted to the darkness, then Professor Jouan pointed almost directly overhead and said:

" 'If you look closely, you'll see a bright object where I'm pointing. It may look to you like a little comet, or perhaps, a sort of mist—depending upon your eyes. Do you observe it?'

" 'Yes,' Maria and I said.

" 'That, my friends, is the island universe Andromeda. It is composed of at least a *million* suns, and is about one *million* light years from us. Andromeda's suns rotate about a common center, and that rotation requires about seventeen *million* years. Now, observe again, that beyond Andromeda, are *millions* of such island universes—all of them contain *millions* of suns!'

"The professor continued. 'And the end is not yet, for only recently, modern telescopes have revealed that we've reached, comparatively speaking, but a few yards into space. Is not God's boundless ocean of starry universes overwhelming to contemplate, Madam?'

"Maria, sitting with hunched shoulders, stared at the floor and did not answer. 'Oh,' the professor said contritely, 'I have wearied you. This I regret, madam, for I . . .'

" 'No, no,' Maria said quickly, 'you have not wearied me, monsieur. It's only that I am overcome with a sad thought. Compared with the vastness of God's worlds, we humans on earth are small—so small, perhaps, that it could be easy for God to forget us. I know, Professor, that this is a wrong thought, yet it came to me and I have been praying, while you talked, that God will enable me to understand why He loves such bits of—of almost nothing—among the stars.'

" 'That is a thought that comes to all when they first study God's great works, madam,' the professor said. But we soon learn that to God, nothing is large and nothing is small. We learn that for God there is no time, nor space, nor distance; He is *all*—and all *time* is *now* to God. As to smallness, madam, again I ask you to observe:

" 'The *billions* upon *billions* of suns composing the *millions* upon *millions* of island universes are composed of atoms—as are all other material things in the Heavens and upon earth. Atoms are composed of only two things: nuclei and electrons. The nuclei are like tiny suns, around which the electrons orbit exactly like planets. Indeed, they are infinitesimally small solar systems almost identical with our own solar system. Atoms are so small that it would require all of the people in the world—counting as fast as they could—sixteen *million* years to count the atoms in the first joint of your little finger.

" 'Recall, my friends, I have said that the atom is made of only two things—a nucleus, and electrons. I also told you that everything in Heaven and earth—of a material nature—is composed of atoms—atoms only. Note, then, that God made all material things: stars, earth, animals, rocks, waters, plants, air, clouds—everything—from only two things: nucleons (which are atomic nuclei) and electrons. Only two things to make an infinity of forms—yet, no two forms on the earth or in the skies are precisely alike.'

"Professor Jouan paused a moment, as if gathering his facts, then went on:

" 'The stars obey God's Law because He wills them to.

" 'The atoms obey God's Law because He wills them to.

" 'His infinite creations obey His Laws because He wills them to.

" 'Only *man* is different.

" 'Only to man has the Creator given the godlike attributes of mind and free will.

" 'Only man may *choose* whether or not he will obey God's Laws.

" 'And that man may ever know which is God's Way, he has been given prayer.'

"The professor turned to Maria. 'And so, *ma chère*' he said. 'You see that Man is God's greatest creation.' "

The rest of Albert's story, Professor Jouan told me later. He said:

"Albert Flamin had a unique mind and he learned quickly. Within one year, he was reading astronomy. His umbrella business grew steadily. Then they sold the right to the constellation design to a manufacturer of sunshades, and the design was soon seen by the thousands on the beaches of Belgium, France and Holland. Albert became a stockholder in the Sunshade Company, and within five years, was able to restore the hamlet in which he was born. He and Maria regained full health, and now Albert is writing a book of what the stars have taught him of God. The title of the book, *Tabernacle in the Sky,* was taken from the nineteenth psalm, the first verse of which begins:

"The Heavens declare the glory of God."

THE MANUSCRIPT of "God's Ranch in Pleasant Valley," submitted to a man who has been teaching philosophy in American colleges for more than thirty years, with the request that he comment, brought this brief reply:

"In the main, philosophy graduates are the most confused of America's confused young men. Within a year after receiving their degrees, many of them cannot define intelligently such disciplines as ontology, cosmology, theology, esthetics, psychology, epistemology, logic and ethics, nor have they any clear idea of the soul, or of God.

"In part, this confusion arises from the fact that many philosophers suffered from one or more personality defects such as eccentricity (Schopenhauer), emotional instability, perversity of conduct, undue conceit (Nietzsche), oversuspiciousness, lack of common sense, etc., and in the case of one American philosopher—downright silliness.

"Now these personality defects, taken together, are the symptoms of insanity. That is why the combined works of these men, absorbed in toto by immature minds, come out again as confusion confounded.

"While not a few modern philosophers believed in God—Descartes, Spinoza, Leibniz, Kant, Fechner, Hobbes, Locke, Fichte—they tried, in some cases, to disassociate God from His works—which is attempting to disassociate the parts from the whole.

"I think, perhaps, the Schlick brothers of the God's Ranch story arrived at a philosophical concept similar to that of Britain's Alexander, namely:

"The world with its striving (nisus) toward deity stirs

in us a longing for God with whom we are in communion. And practical religion consists in doing our duty so as to advance the progress of the world towards deity.

"I agree with the Schlicks that the half-baked understanding of philosophy with which many of our graduates leave school gives the graduate nothing."

God's Ranch in Pleasant Valley

ONE DAY IN 1955 WHILE EATING LUNCH IN THE RES-taurant on the RKO-Pathé lot in Culver City, California, I overheard part of a discussion going on at the next table about what I thought was a projected movie to be called: "God's Ranch in Pleasant Valley." The idea of God's Ranch intrigued me, and later I asked a producer if he knew who was making the picture. He said:

" 'God's Ranch in Pleasant Valley' isn't a movie script—it's an answer-to-prayer story. Seems the story's about a couple of writers named Schlick. They're clients of the Paul Kohner Agency."

At Kohner's, Ilse Lahn, clients' executive, told me that the Schlicks were Frederick and Robert, twins, and that their prayer story was one of the most inspiring she'd heard. "They're at their ranch in Pleasant Valley now," she said.

"God's Ranch?"

"Yes," she said, and gave me directions for driving to it.

The narrow road north of Phoenix, on which, two days later, I drove through one of America's most primitive areas—Arizona's Tonto Basin—twisted up steep mountain grades, hugged canyon rims, wound through forests, bridged mountain streams, and about an hour before sunset, led me to a small church in the drowsy hamlet of Pleasant Valley.

Wide-open doors of the church promised coolness inside and I went in to rest a few minutes before driving on to the general store to inquire my way to the Schlicks' ranch. However, from a scaffold that stretched along the church's back wall, a small, sprightly, gray-haired woman wearing an artist's smock smiled down at me. Apparently she'd just put the finishing touches on a colorful scenic mural that covered the back wall, for she was covering cans of paint and stacking them near the edge of the scaffold.

"Howdy, Stranger," she said.

"That mural gives one the feeling that the church is open to the outdoors," I said.

"God made this country beautiful," she said, "and I thought it a shame to shut it out with a concrete wall, so I've tried to bring some of the beauty inside."

"Somewhere in this neighborhood is a prayer story about a ranch I've heard spoken of as 'God's Ranch.' I collect prayer stories; I'd like to write this one. Can you direct me?"

"I live there," she said.

"With Frederick and Robert Schlick?"

"Yes. I'm their mother."

"And you know their prayer story?"

"Of course. It's my prayer story, too, you see. Each evening the boys drive in from the ranch to pick me up. They should be here any minute now. It's quite a story, so you'd better plan on staying overnight with us."

Frederick and Robert proved to be in their mid-forties, and although they were twins, Frederick was blond, Robert dark. Both had attended colleges in the

United States, Europe and Mexico. Both had doctorates in philosophy.

With their mother—whom they called Dodie—beside me on the front seat of my car, I followed the Schlick boys in their Lincoln, and not long after leaving the church, we stopped on the crest of a forested mountain to look down into a miniature canyon valley.

"Down there," Frederick said, "is our answer to prayer—the prettiest little ranch in this whole country. A creek runs through it, and, as you see, it's embraced by pine-covered mountains. The house, the barn, the cottage, the windmill, the cow, chickens and everything else on the place came to us as an answer to prayer."

"And along with those practical things," Robert said, "for good measure, God gave us the shrubs, the wild flowers, the birds' songs and flashing colors, the cloud shadows that scud across the fields, the sunshine and rain, the tadpoles and minnows in the creek, the spider webs that lace the fence corners, the bear, the deer, the mountain lions and wild turkeys that take shelter on the hill slopes—everything."

"Yes," Dodie said, "everything. The moonlight, the crying of night birds, the laughter of the creek, the silver of its waters, the glorious sunrises and sunsets. We call our ranch God's Ranch—not only because He helped us acquire it, but because it's so rich with His blessings."

"This seems strange talk from two doctors of philosophy," I said.

"You won't think it strange after you hear our story," Frederick said.

With the cars in low gear, we eased down the steep grades to the valley floor where a red-and-white cow, chewing on a discarded tennis shoe, greeted us by dropping the shoe and bawling. As Dodie stepped from my car beside the weathered ranch house, three cats joyously rubbed themselves against her ankles, and from the kitchen doorway, Frederick's wife March—a blonde with smiling eyes—greeted us with the news that supper would be on the table in a few minutes. The sun began to sink behind the hills, and we all paused on the porch to watch twilight fill the valley. It was like a benediction.

We ate in the kitchen by lamplight, and when the table had been cleared, we gathered around it to listen to Frederick tell the story of the ranch.

"While Robert and I were still in grammar school," he said, "we agreed we'd follow writing careers, and that when success came, we'd buy a ranch far from the noises, grime and smells of big cities. Through high school and college we followed a stern course of reading and study—our aim to be writers never wavering, our dream of a ranch always growing brighter.

"The money our parents had set aside for our education was exhausted by the time we received our doctorates, and to finance or writing, we worked at whatever we could find to do—as warehousemen, clerks, butlers, laborers—and, on occasion, radio script writers. When we'd saved a sizable stake, we would hole up in inexpensive quarters and write industriously. We attained success of a kind—my first play *Bloodstream* was produced on Broadway; Robert's first book, a collection of poems, was published.

"Neither venture made much money, though, and we returned to the grind of miscellaneous jobs. We'd met several successful writers, and had noted that none of them had any real financial security. They'd write a play, a book or a story, then make a sale and spend the money while hammering out another play, book or story.

"Robert and I feared that unless we undertook a more businesslike program, we, too, would spend our returns as they were earned, and probably never be able to buy our dream ranch. We decided that for the next five years, we'd continue to finance our writing by taking jobs when necessary, and that we'd make no attempts to market our manuscripts until we had a large enough stock of them to enable us to buy our ranch.

"To eliminate any possibility of our writings becoming 'dated' during the five years, we wrote only on subjects of perpetual interest. For instance, I undertook a series of five plays about the lives of great artists—Gauguin, Van Gogh and three of their contemporaries; two novels, a technical book and some short stories. Robert undertook two epic poems, two novels and numerous pastorals, epodes, chorals and dramatic poems.

"Our program took longer to complete than we'd planned—nine years instead of five—but the day finally arrived when our works went out to producers and agents, and because their reports were enthusiastic, Robert and I spent happy weeks of anticipation—counting the chickens from our unhatched eggs.

"Then came World War II, sending Robert to Saipan with the Air Force, and me to Hawaii to work on top-secret reports with the Navy. During the months that followed, Robert and I wrote each other frequently, the gist of our letters being discussions of plans for new after-the-war writing projects which, of course, were to be written at the ranch we would purchase immediately at war's end.

"Never once did we doubt that our work would bring us recognition and pleasing financial returns, and we expected publication and production to be underway before the war ended. That's why we were overwhelmed when a letter arrived informing us that because of paper shortages, publication of our books had been postponed indefinitely; that all five of my plays had been finally rejected.

"I was hurt, bewildered and depressed, and the producer's brief note, arriving a few days later, didn't help. He wrote:

> This war, more than any that America has fought heretofore, is causing a spiritual revolution among the People, and it will grow more manifest during a long postwar period. Books and plays during the coming years must have spiritual significance if they're to be highly successful. Rewrite your plays, Frederick, adding depth, and some measure of spirituality. It was really lack of true spirituality in the lives of Van Gogh and Gauguin that destroyed them, you know.

"How easy, I thought, for someone to say 'rewrite your five plays!' And did one add spirituality to a play as a cook adds pepper to soup? I crumpled the letter and threw it into the wastebasket.

"During the following weeks I passed through periods of resentment, disillusionment, self-pity, depression and despair. And I knew that Robert, because he was my twin, was having an identical experience. To make matters worse, I'd turned to the philosophers for direction and solace, and had found they had none to offer. I became convinced that philosophy, as Colton once said, was 'a bully that talked very loud when danger was at a distance, but the moment she was hard pressed by the enemy she was not to be found at her post.'

"And Colton had added that philosophy left the brunt of the battle to be borne by her humbler and steadier comrade, religion.

"Religion! The word struck a spark. How long since I'd thought seriously about it! As children, Robert and I had said morning and evening prayers, and we'd had absolute faith that God heard—and answered. Would things have been different now had we retained our simple faith? Had too much philosophy led us down a dark road? Philosophy. The word now brought back a memory, something my father had read aloud from the Bible when I was too young to understand.

"I went to the post library, opened a concordance, looked up the word 'philosophy,' ran my eyes down the column and paused at the notation: Colossians 2:8. I took a Bible from a shelf and read St. Paul's admonition:

> *Beware lest any man spoil you through philosophy and vain deceit, after the tradition of men, after the elements of the world, and not after Christ.*

"Philosophy! The actual meaning of the word was 'love of wisdom,' and wisdom was, essentially, 'knowledge of what is true and right.' With that thought came a sense of elation, as though I were on the verge of a great discovery. And I was—for a few minutes later, I began reading Colossians 2:2, 3, and there it was:

> *That their hearts might be comforted, being knit together in love, and to all riches of the full assurance of understanding, to the acknowledgement of the mystery of God, and of the Father, and of Christ;*
> *In whom are hid all the treasures of wisdom and knowledge.*

"That night, in a letter to Robert I said I'd learned from those words, written by Paul two thousand years ago, what six years of college had been unable to teach me—that the search for wisdom and knowledge is a search for God, and therefore, any philosophy that didn't point the student toward God was false.

"During the following months, through study of the New Testament—particularly the words of Jesus—Robert and I were able to discard the fallacious findings of philosophers, and replace them with the beauty and truth of Christ's teachings. With the coming of this transformation in our thinking, our bitterness and sense of failure regarding our writings left us, and we placed our work in His hands to be held, abandoned or rewritten, as He directed.

"The only income Robert and I had at this time was our military pay, and at war's end, all we'd have with which to begin civilian life would be our discharge pay of three hundred dollars each. Jobs, we believed, would be few and hard to find because of the millions of men to be released from service. This problem was dismaying for a while, but it, too, we placed in God's hands.

"Came a day when our faith was so strengthened that we asked God to help us obtain the ranch we'd dreamed of for so long. I remember that in praying for a ranch, I said: 'You've promised those who follow You in love that they shall have every good thing. We believe that a ranch is good for us—something we seem to need. Of ourselves, with no money, such a purchase would be impossible, but we believe that with Your aid, even that obstacle will be overcome. We pray in faith.'

"Two days later an astonishing chain of events began that finally led us to this delightful home of ours—God's Ranch in Pleasant Valley.

"Robert and I had never definitely decided just where we'd like the ranch to be, so we asked God to help us decide that. Shortly thereafter, I became engrossed in a book by Zane Grey—*To the Last Man*—the setting of which was the Tonto Basin country of Arizona. Grey's descriptions of climate and primitive grandeur fascinated

me, and I sent Robert a copy of the book, asking him
to read it and let me know if he'd like our ranch to be
in the Tonto Basin. He sent me an enthusiastic 'yes.'

"Thereupon, I wrote the Department of Interior for
topographical and other maps of the entire Tonto Basin
and Mogollon Rim country; and the local forest ranger
in Pleasant Valley, for prices of ranch land, rainfall and
other general information. When a month later the maps
arrived, I hung a detailed forestry map on the wall over
my desk.

"Within one week, in walked a captain of the Navy
who'd spent a couple of years in that wild country,
putting in roads for the government. He knew the country well, and his descriptions thrilled me. Out of the
millions of men in the Navy, probably not more than
a dozen had ever been in the Tonto country, and that
one of them should happen to spy the map on my wall,
and recognize it, was beyond the realm of mere chance.

"The fact that Robert and I weren't cowboys, miners
or loggers—and the only possible jobs in the Tonto
Basin were in cattle, lumber or mining—meant that if
we got a ranch there, our income would depend solely
on our writing. So we reasoned that if God made a ranch
available, He would mean us to write. Just how much
income this would bring us we had no idea, but we
had faith!

"A year passed, and most of the next, and then we
were back in the States; and with the end of the war, we
were discharged from the service—Bobbie with his
three hundred dollars, I with mine. We promptly invited friends to our apartment to a party in order to
announce that we were leaving New York for Arizona
in about three months, 'to buy a small ranch.' It was a
fine evening.

"Then, entirely unexpectedly, I had an offer to write
a series of coast-to-coast radio dramas for N.B.C.—

providing I wrote the first one successfully. It was not until after I had done so that N.B.C. told me that seventeen other writers had failed on the initial script.

"In any event, having written the first dramatic program, I followed through with others, one after another. These programs took about ten days apiece to write, and paid two hundred and fifty dollars each. When I'd saved one thousand dollars, Bobbie and I figured it was time to start for Arizona. Cars were hard to buy in those days just after the war, but we finally found a Lincoln Zephyr in perfect condition, and plunked down five hundred dollars as a down payment. How we could pay the monthly payments (which were considerable) we didn't know. We only knew that somehow everything would work out all right.

"The following day we packed, and that night, in a driving rainstorm, about midnight, with Mother, March, our three cats and ourselves—and the car loaded down with suitcases and bedding—we headed along the glittering streets of Manhattan, ducked under the Hudson River via the Holland Tunnel and shot out along the Pulaski Skyway. Dawn found us in Virginia. Ten days later, we climbed the narrow mountain road leading up from the Arizona Desert into the forest country. By this time we had only three hundred dollars left in actual cash, but continued to feel completely undaunted. At sunset, we got our first sight of Pleasant Valley, several thousand feet below and several miles beyond. And it seemed to us like the Promised Land.

"For two weeks, we lived in some cabins of a ranch-woman who rented them and served our meals. And for two weeks each day, we drove miles in and around the valley to inspect various ranches for sale. One we liked cost one hundred and forty thousand dollars! Another, sixty thousand dollars. And by this time, we were down to about one hundred and fifty dollars. Our faith was being severely tested, but we remained enthusiastic. The country was everything we'd wished for—and more.

"Then one day I stopped at a country store in Pleasant Valley for gasoline, and Bobbie went in for a cup of coffee. An elderly, retired rancher named Uncle Buck asked Bobbie if we'd seen the old Peverly ranch. He said it wasn't any great shakes, but was what he considered the prettiest little ranch in the country, and that he thought it could be bought cheap.

"Next morning we located it, and loved all of its forty acres—for they constituted a miniature canyon valley of their own. The owner, an old-timer, lived in Phoenix, and the ranch was in the care of one of the local ranchers. From him we received permission to move into the cabin. We wrote and told the owner we'd done so, and were interested in perhaps buying his ranch. A week later, the old gentleman arrived. He agreed to give me a six-month option to buy, in return for only twenty-five dollars. This we did.

"Again, out of the clear blue sky arrived an airmail letter from N.B.C. in New York asking if I'd continue writing additional half-hour radio dramas for their program. Over the forest ranger's telephone line (the only telephone line in that part of the country) I sent a telegram of eager acceptance.

"As though that weren't enough, a month or so after that, while busy writing radio scripts, an offer came from Hollywood to do a screen play there. This I accepted.

"The upshot was that three months after we'd moved onto the little ranch, I was able to pay for the ranch in full. And six months later, I returned from Hollywood with sufficient money to make all of the improvements we'd envisioned—a new windmill for the well and additional rooms and porches on the cabin. And there was enough money left over to last us comfortably for several years.

"We'll never sell this ranch—for to us, it's the concrete manifestation of the power of prayer."

Frederick paused a moment, then added:

"Faith is the key to answered prayer. I think it might be helpful to your readers if you quoted Robert Hall":

> Faith is a practical habit, which like every other, is strengthened and increased by continual exercise. It is nourished by meditation, by prayer, and the devout perusal of the Scriptures.

"Yes, I'll include that," I said. "Now tell me what happened to your books and plays."

"Two of the books have been published since we bought the ranch," he said, "and the plays, after much prayer, are being rewritten."

Next morning, as I headed back to Hollywood, I stopped my car on top of the mountain from which I'd first seen God's Ranch. The smoke from the kitchen chimney rose in a blue-white pillar—as if from an altar.

"HOW ARE YOU able to find so many stories of answered prayer?"

That is the question most frequently asked me by readers. So many request this information that from time to time I get out a mimeographed letter on which is a note explaining that it would be physically impossible for me to answer, individually, all who inquire. The latest of those mimeographed letters follows:

NOT LONG AGO, having business with the James Transfer and Storage Company of San Jose, California, I stood at a counter in a spacious office, impressed by the air of serenity that pervaded the place. The clerk who waited on me was courteous and helpful. The warehousemen to whom I was sent for further information seemed to enjoy answering my questions even though I was interrupting their work. Back in the office again, I said I'd like to talk to Mr. W. Ray James, the proprietor, and was promptly ushered into his office. I said:

Mr. James, whenever I enter a business house where clerks are cheerful, helpful, kindly and efficient—where the atmosphere is one of serenity and prosperity—I know that somewhere in the management of that organization is a man who prays. Are you a praying man?"

"He smiled, waved an arm to include all of his large, several-storied building, and said:

"I owe every stick and stone and brick in this building to prayer. I owe its growth to prayer, and I owe its prosperity to prayer."

HOLLISTER IS THE name of a prosperous little

town in a fertile hidden valley in San Benito County, California. Hollister is noted for its clean, shaded streets; as the shipping point for high-quality walnuts, apricots, and cattle; and as the home of a thirty-five-year-old Italian-American shoemaker named Paul Bruno. "Take your shoes to Paul's," Hollister people say, "and you'll always get something extra—a free shine, new laces—and inspiration."

Bruno's shop was small, but clean and shining. He stopped his whirring buffing machine to come to the counter and smile at me. "I hear so many good things about you, Mr. Bruno," I said, "that I'm sure you must be a praying man."

"Sure," he said, "I pray plenty."

"Asking God to help you? Make you prosperous?"

"Oh, sure. But mostly, I pray for the other fellow."

"What other fellow?"

"Oh, you, and . . ." He pointed out the window at two passing men. "And him, and him. And for people who come to my shop, and for people who go to other men's shops."

"And praying makes you happy?"

"Oh, sure. My girl is president of the eighth grade class. My wife loves me. Everybody is my friend. A man comes to my shop, and I say to myself: 'Paul, this man must leave here happier than when he came.' So I pray: 'God, make me say the right thing to make this man happy.' So God helps me to say it."

"And you make good money?"

"Sure. But kindness makes people happier than money. Who wants a lot of money? Kindness, that is best."

IN BROOKINGS, OREGON, are two men named Dimmick, who operate a large market. Here, as at James Transfer and Storage, the atmosphere is one of *serenity, and employees are eager to please. The Dimmicks' hearts and pocketbooks are always open to the truly needy; no man knows how many they help, for their giving is in secret. Praying men, the Dimmicks— like tens of thousands of other small businessmen throughout the country.*

IN HOLLYWOOD, WHERE I spend a lot of time, are two kinds of movie stars—those who pray and those who don't. Praying stars, such as Lew Ayers, Dale Evans, Roy Rogers, Mala Powers, Smiley Burnett and Loretta Young—and at least fifty others—are kindly, helpful, considerate persons leading worthwhile, constructive lives. Their first thoughts are always for others. Their names are never connected with scandal, nor will they permit dreamed-up publicity stories to be written about them. All have experienced miraculous answers to prayer, and all are generous with outpourings of love for the unfortunate. Someday I'll write their prayer stories—particularly that of Smiley Burnett and his wife, who have taken at least seven handicapped children into their home and hearts.

IN BUSINESS, IN entertainment, in politics, in law enforcement, in medicine—in all walks of life—are untold millions of stories of answered prayer. To find them, look for benevolence, kindness, charity, warmheartedness, sympathy, understanding, tenderness and love. When you see these things in a man or woman, you've found a man or woman who prays truly.

Each Today We Share With God

Twenty-five-year-old Herman van der Byl stood in the warehouse of his Johannesburg, South Africa, bicycle shop surrounded by jumbled heaps of warped and twisted wooden-rimmed bicycle wheels. The bicycles had been imported from America with capital he'd raised by mortgaging everything in his store and shop, including his tools. The wooden rims, unable to stand up in the dryness and heat of the South African climate, could not be made salable. Herman might have salvaged most of his investment by substituting steel rims, but his bank refused to lend additional money. In this one unfortunate deal, Herman's efforts and his dreams had gone up in smoke—he was broke.

More was involved, however, than the loss of the business he'd built up during the past five years. For one thing, he'd been so sure that his introduction of American-made bicycles would be a successful venture that he'd persuaded Virginia Mueller, his long-time sweetheart, to set a wedding date. Now, without money to even pay his rent, marriage, too, had become a shattered dream.

Standing there among those tortured wheels, Herman tried to understand why his hard work and high hopes had ended in failure. Five years of unremitting effort should have enabled him to accumulate a sufficient cash reserve to tide him over an occasional deal that went bad. His first year in business had been reasonably profitable; he'd featured children's bikes, but because children liked to hang around his shop and ask questions and handle his tools, his customers were sometimes annoyed. So he had dropped "kids" business and concentrated on adult lines.

He'd made some mistakes. Some were due to lack of experience; others because of his propensity for picking up "bargains." One such deal—the purchase of one thousand "bargain" tires that on delivery were found to have deteriorated in storage—had set him back on his financial heels. Yet despite occasional slip-ups, the business had thrived moderately until a competitor had moved in across the street. From then on, Herman had done well to break even.

Almost everyone in South Africa rides a bicycle, including natives. And as natives outnumber Europeans ten to one, the native trade is eagerly sought. And although Herman got his share, it was not enough to lift his business from its rut.

Like other bicycle dealers in South Africa, Herman had been selling British-made bikes—good jobs, but invariably painted black, a color that pleased the conservative tastes of Britishers, but had small appeal for natives.

Herman had spent many hours—particularly in bed at night—trying to figure out some method or scheme for increasing his sales to natives, but without success. Then one day when he stepped from his store to find the first American-made bike he'd ever seen parked on the sidewalk, he thought he'd found the answer. The bike was red, with bright nickel fittings, and it was surrounded by natives excitedly admiring its brilliant color. Herman decided to try to corner the native bicycle market by importing colored bikes from America—greens, reds, blues, yellows, even purple ones, for Africans dearly love purple.

His idea seemed good to his banker, and the banker lent Herman a sufficient amount of money to import three hundred brightly enameled bicycles from Wisconsin. Herman had assumed that American bikes, like British ones, would come with steel rims. Instead, his shipment came equipped with wooden ones.

Wishing to clean out his British line before introducing the new American one, Herman stored the bikes in a hot, dry galvanized-iron warehouse. During the rainy season, the warehouse became humid, and within weeks every rim had buckled.

When Herman asked his banker for a loan that would enable him to substitute steel rims, the banker refused. "Steel rims," he told Herman, "would make those bicycles salable, but they'd eat up all the profit. In fact, it appears we'll have to take a loss no matter what we do. *You* can't afford such a loss, and we won't—so the bank will take over those bikes. We'll do our best to get a price for them that won't leave you owing us a great amount of money. And it may be," he added in a more kindly tone, "that this transaction will teach you the need of investigating thoroughly before plunging into things."

And so it was that Herman now stood humiliated and discouraged among six hundred useless bicycle wheels. So intent was he on his misery that he wasn't aware of Virginia observing him from the warehouse doorway until she said:

"Troubles, Herman?"

"Plenty," he said, and pointed to the rims surrounding him. "There, Virginia, lie our hopes of an early marriage. The bank won't finance me any longer. I'm broke."

"I've known for some time that you were having business worries, Herman. I've been praying for you."

"Well," he said testily, "if going broke is the answer to your prayers, I don't . . ."

"Herman, Herman! Listen! You haven't gone broke."

"No? Well, what do you call it when the bank takes over your merchandise? When you can't pay your bills —not even the rent? What do you call it when years of effort go down the drain?"

"As I see it, Herman, only a *phase* of your business career has ended. You've still got most of the things you started business with—your health, your youth, your mechanical ability, your imagination. What have you lost except money?"

"My credit, for one thing."

"Only temporarily. It will be better than ever when you get paid up."

"I've lost faith in myself, my plans for the future, my ideas . . ."

"Maybe it's because you left God out of your plans, Herman. Have you been happy selling bicycles?"

"I was a lot happier in the old days when I was dealing with kids. But . . ."

"Will you pray *with* me, Herman?"

"Now? Here?"

"Yes. Here and now."

"I didn't ask God for help when I was doing well, and I certainly am not going to make a beggar of myself and ask Him for help now when I'm down and out. Anyway, I've no faith in prayer—in my own prayers, I mean."

"But you come from a praying family, Herman!"

"Sure—both Mother and Father prayed, but not for business, not for material things."

"You remember your mother's prayers?"

"Of course. She prayed for God's help and guidance —for herself, her children, for all things. I never heard her pray for things of a material nature."

"Probably not—for your mother undoubtedly remembered that Jesus said: . . . *your Father knoweth what things ye have need of before ye ask Him.* I think your mother prayed rightly. You see, Herman, if we have God's guidance, we don't have to ask for *things,* for God will guide us to everything that's good for us. In my prayers for you, I don't ask God to save your business or to bring you wealth. I simply ask that He guide you. Will you pray that prayer with me Herman? Now?"

"No," he said. "I've told you how I feel about it. And stop preaching at me. I'll make good on my own. Anyway, I've already told you I've no faith."

"That's all right, Herman. I've enough faith for both," Virginia said as she moved to the door. She paused to add: "I'll be praying for you, Herman, so from now on, you may be sure that God is working *with* you." She smiled at him briefly and walked off down the street.

The rest of this story is best told in Herman's own words, taken from notes I made in 1939 when I interviewed him at San Francisco where he was the South African delegate to an international post-polio rehabilitation conference.

"I was irritated by Virginia's presumption that I wasn't man enough to make good without going to my knees, but at the same time, I was sorry that my attitude toward prayer made her unhappy. Anyway, all I needed was enough new capital to re-establish the business, and I couldn't imagine asking God to help me raise money. I decided that one thousand pounds was the amount I needed, and set out grimly determined to borrow them.

"My requests for loans were unhesitatingly turned down by Johannesburg's four banks. I then approached several friends, but none was interested in my proposals. The last one I called on said:

" 'Look, Herman, you're a good mechanic. Why

don't you get a job in some garage, and leave business to those who are more practical?'

" 'You think I'm impractical? Is that why you turned me down?'

" 'South Africa's bicycle business is booming. Your competitors are growing and expanding, but you've lost ground because you've been interested in impractical get-rich-quick deals rather than in good, solid business procedures. At any rate, that's how your friends see it.'

" 'So that's it,' I said bitterly. 'Just because I show a little imagination . . .'

" 'The Chevrolet people need men,' he interrupted. 'I'll be glad to give you a letter of reference.'

" 'Go to the devil,' I said, and walked away.

" 'It's true,' I told Virginia that evening. 'I could get a job at good wages as a garage mechanic, but don't you see that taking a job would be admitting I'm a failure as a businessman? Now, more than ever, I've got to get back into business and make good to show my friends —to show the banks—to retain my self-respect.'

" 'I understand you very well, Herman. But you don't understand yourself. You *are* impractical, you know.'

" 'You, too!' I said morosely.

" 'Oh, Herman, don't you see that your real interest is not in selling bicycles, but in the promotion of your imaginative ideas? Those beautifully painted bikes from America, for instance. That was—it still is—a novel and practical idea. But it failed. Why? Not because the idea wasn't good, but because you let the manufacturer ship you wooden rims. That's where the impractical part comes in. The lovely colors of those bicycles blinded you to the practical side of the venture.'

" 'But how was I to know they wouldn't come with steel rims?'

" 'A good businessman would have checked that. Then, there was your scheme for . . .'"

" 'That's enough,' I said shortly.

"Virginia sighed, and we both were thoughtful for some time. Then she said:

" 'You had a prosperous and happy business when you were dealing with children, Herman. It wasn't until you dropped the kids and concentrated on adult business that you began to slip. Children flocked to your shop. Do you know why? Because you *loved* them, and entered into their imaginative world with them. You helped them name their bicycles. I still smile when I recall some of those names—Smoothy, Hortense, John Gilpin. And one that was named after a little girl's doll—Alice Blue. Remember, Herman? And you told them stories, wonderfully imaginative stories. Your bikes weren't any better than those of your competitors, Herman. So it wasn't your wares that attracted the children—it was *you*. They *knew* you were interested in *them*. They loved to visit your shop. You've a talent for making children happy.'

"The revelation in Virginia's words acted on my heart like a clean, fresh wind. The confusion, resentments and bitterness that had darkened my outlook seemed to blow away, and their places were taken by a sense of freedom, a gladness. I said:

" 'I'm beginning to understand, Virginia. Why have you waited so long to tell me these things?'

" 'I wanted to say them,' she said. 'I even tried to. But you told me not to preach at you, and I knew that you weren't ready for the truth. So I prayed—and waited.'

" 'You know, Virginia,' I told her, 'when I said I didn't have faith in prayer, I wasn't telling the truth. I felt the need of prayer even as you talked of it, but resented that need. I think what I was doing was taking out on God my exasperation with myself.'

" 'I sensed that too, darling,' Virginia said.

"Without another word, we knelt beside one another.

" 'Forgive me, God,' I said, 'and please show me the way.'

" 'Show us both the way, Father,' Virginia said.

"It wasn't until we started to get to our feet that I noticed we'd been holding hands.

"Shortly after Virginia left, I began wondering *why* God should help me. My financial situation wasn't too bad. None had lost any money but myself, not even the bank. The thousand pounds I needed to start again wasn't much of a sum for a single man to save if he went to work as a mechanic—so asking God to help me financially seemed absurd. The exaltation I'd felt after praying diminished. And then I realized that Virginia and I hadn't prayed for financial help, but for guidance —to be shown the Way.

"My spirits lifted and I knew for a certainty that if I could find the Way, all good things would be mine, including financial security. To follow it safely, I needed guidance. Silently I told God I'd wait for His direction.

"What had I done that was wrong, that was out of harmony with God's plans for me? Was it that I'd tried to walk alone? The children! Had it been wrong for me to abandon them? Virginia had said I had a talent with children. Talent! An aptitude? A capacity? I wasn't sure, so I rummaged through my desk drawers until I found a long-unused office dictionary, and read this:

> Talent, noun. The abilities, powers and gifts bestowed upon a man, natural endowments;— thought of as a Divine trust.

"Talents! A Divine trust! God-given abilities, powers and gifts! How had I used mine? Had I put them to work to increase them, as had the good servants in Jesus' parable of the talents, or had I buried them as had the fearful servant? In this moment of revelation I *knew* that if Man utilized his talents to the best of his abilities, financial security, and the respect of his fellow men would fall to him naturally. What were my own talents that God wanted me to use? I wasn't sure, so I prayed that God would reveal them to me.

"My prayer was answered two days later, although at the time I didn't recognize it as an answer to prayer.

"I'd just returned from lunch that day when a physician named Spring entered the store and asked if I had a secondhand bicycle for a child. I told him I hadn't. He didn't answer at once, but walked over to the display of mortgaged bikes, looked one over carefully, tested the pedals and said:

" 'Well, it doesn't matter—it was an impossible idea, anyway.'

" 'If you'll go across the street to my competitor, you'll probably find what you want,' I said.

"He sighed, seeming suddenly weary. I pushed a chair toward him and he sat down. 'It was just an idea,' he said. 'I see now that it won't work.'

" 'I don't understand, Doctor,' I said.

" 'I'm a physician in the slums of Vrededorp,' he said. 'I've two children—patients—recovering from infantile paralysis. They require special exercises for their legs if they're to walk again, and the other day I got the idea that if they were able to pedal bicycles—not actually riding them, but pedaling from a stationary stand—it would be just the thing. Easy as these bikes are to pedal, however, I see now that they'd be beyond the strength of wasted muscles.' He smiled sadly and went on. 'And I probably couldn't afford even an inexpensive bike. Slum doctors make little money, you know.' He stood up to leave.

" 'Wait,' I said impulsively. 'Maybe I can do some-

thing. Maybe I can rig up a bicycle that would practically pedal itself. Could you bring one of those children in
so I can see what's needed?'

"He didn't answer—just looked at me.

" 'Please,' I said.

"He still didn't answer, but at the door as he left, he
said:

" 'May God be good to you, my friend. I'll bring one
of the children tomorrow.'

"The next afternoon I met little Jessie MacClintock.
She was six years old, with dark wavy hair and black-
lashed, dancing blue-gray eyes. She wore a stiffly
starched white-and-pink-checked pinafore over a dark-
blue wool dress. Her wasted legs were in steel braces.
Dr. Spring carried her to a chair and seated her carefully.

" 'Now don't wiggle, Jessie,' he said. 'I don't want
you falling off.' Then he turned to me.

" 'Let me explain,' he said, 'that my ideas of exercise
and massage for cases such as Jessie's is frowned upon
by most physicians of this area. Rather than exercise or
manipulate the degenerated muscles, they try to prevent
all movement of them by encasing the legs in plaster of
Paris casts. For some time, I've been convinced that
such casts do no good, and I've had a measure of success by employing judicious exercises.

" 'But I'm a busy physician, with little spare time and
little spare money. I've prayed God would show me a
way to exercise those pitiful little legs in some manner
that would permit me to go about my work while the
exercises went on. It was shortly after such a prayer that
the idea of a bicycle came to me. It seemed just the thing.
But . . .'

" 'You said you'd like a bike that would practically
"wheel" itself, Doctor. In other words, a back wheel

that would push the pedals once it had begun to re-
volve. Did I understand correctly?'

" 'Something like that.'

" 'Well, I, too, prayed after you left. And I'm quite
sure I can build a bike that will be what you want. Jessie's small for her age, and I haven't a bike right here
that'll do, but I think I know where to get one. If you'll
bring Jessie back again tomorrow afternoon, I'll have a
surprise for you.'

" 'Don't go to too much expense,' Dr. Spring said.
'I'm really not in a position to . . .'

" 'There'll be no expense at all to you, Doctor,' I
said.

"When the doctor and Jessie had gone, I rummaged
through a pile of rusted, discarded bicycle parts that lay
in the back yard, and came up with an old frame, two
wheels, a seat bracket and a pair of badly bent handle
bars. In fact, I salvaged enough parts to make a bike,
requiring only tires, handle bar grips, roller chain, a seat
and a few spokes to make it complete. I called the bank,
got permission to buy those things from my mortgaged
stock and set to work. I rubbed all the rusted parts
down with emery cloth, finishing them off with a stiff
pumice rub. I enameled the frame green, trued the
wheels, cleaned the ball bearings, and next morning, I
assembled a bike that was just the thing for a ten-year-
old boy.

"Then I trundled the bike out to the home of a family
that had bought a bike for a six-year-old from me four
years before, and traded the larger bike for the small
one. I was back in the shop by lunch time, but I became
so interested in what I was doing that I forgot about
eating.

"I cleaned, oiled and polished the little bike, then
melted lead and poured a series of weights that I could
fasten to the spokes of the back wheel in such a way

that they would not interfere. I secured the bike on two standard bicycle stands, fastened the stands to the floor, stepped back, took out my watch and whirled the pedals. The balanced, weighted back wheel spun merrily on for almost five minutes. I adjusted the weights, spun the pedals again, and after three minutes, grasped a pedal to stop the movement. The wheel stopped spinning under protest.

"When Dr. Spring and Jessie arrived a little later, the bike stood shimmering in a wide beam of sunlight. The doctor removed Jessie's braces, placed her on the bicycle seat and put each foot on a pedal. Then he lifted the little girl down again, and said,

" 'She'll need some sort of stirrup to keep her feet on the pedals; she has no muscular control below the waist.'

"I made adjustable straps from webbed belting, and again the doctor put Jessie on the seat. Then after making sure that her hands were firmly on the handle bar grips, he gave one pedal a gentle downward push. Jessie squealed with delight as her legs began their circling movements. Dr. Spring blew his nose loudly.

"Well, Jessie came every other day for her 'exercises.' That first day, she 'pedaled' about two minutes. Each trip thereafter, the time was increased, and at the end of six weeks she was exercising for from ten to fifteen minutes. One day four months later, by a supreme effort, Jessie started the pedals herself. Dr. Spring's eyes held tears.

"And during those four months, God directed me to go to my competitor across the street and suggest that he buy the American bicycles from the bank, and that the two of us go into partnership. It worked out that way, since he was a good businessman, the business so prospered that Virginia and I were soon able to marry.

"In the meantime, I'd made another exercise bike for

Dr. Spring's boy patient Gilly Smith, and it proved as successful as Jessie's. One day Sir Abe Bailey, a wealthy mining man, sent in a friend whose son's arms and back had been wasted by polio. I rigged up a small row-boat with a flywheel that worked with the boy's back and arms just as the bikes did with Jessie's and Gilly's legs. Later, this boy's father financed me in a business devoted to making special equipment of all kinds for paralysis victims. That business, too, prospered.

"Jessie and Gilly both became entirely normal physically, and Dr. Spring's theory of massage and exercise for post-polio patients is becoming the practice of physicians throughout the world.

"Well, that's my prayer story," Herman concluded. "I sold out both businesses long ago, and Virginia and I devote our time to the physically handicapped. And God has been good to us; we neither fret about the past nor worry about the future. Each morning we repeat:

"God has given us another day in which to do His will. From the past, we bring to this day only what God has taught us. Tomorrow is also God's, and what we do with it depends upon God's guidance. Each today we share with God—and all is well.'

YOU NEED NEVER WALK ALONE

My way was dark, and I walked all alone,
My soul too faint to face those dread tomorrows.
Of Life I'd asked for bread—and got a stone,
My heart was crushed beneath its load of sorrows.
"O God!" I cried, "please lead me into sunlight—
"I dread each troubled night and hopeless day—
"I need Your hand to comfort me and guide me—
"I can no longer walk my stumbling way."

I prayed with tears, and God's clear voice replied:
"Weep not, my child, you need not live with heart-
  ache."
I prayed in trust—now He walks by my side—
I prayed in faith—and joy replaced my heartbreak.
"All Good is yours," God said, "here and in Heaven—
"Forget your fears, my child, for you're my own—
"Whate'er you ask in Love to you is given—
"Pray truly, and you'll never walk alone."

ALEXANDER LAKE

"Why Are Ye Fearful?"

I HEARD MRS. ADELE ECKBERT, NEW YORK TOY MAN-
ufacturer, tell her prayer story at a symposium that had
been called by medical doctors, psychiatrists and television writers, to exchange suggestions on incorporating

spirituality into medical and psychiatric plays. One speaker, Dr. Olin Smith, of Illinois, told us:

"Today, only those medical men who are still living in the nineteenth century will not admit that after medicine and surgery have done all they can for patients, and failed, there is still a spiritual element which, when activated, can, and often does, result in healing. It is this intangible spiritual element that is too often lacking in today's television dramas. Unless you writers can get this spirituality into your stories, you're incompetent."

Dr. Cor Overmeyer, New York state psychiatrist, said:

"Fear in one form or another is the root cause of at least fifty per cent of physical ills, and probably one hundred per cent of mental disturbances. Fear manifests itself in many forms—inability to make decisions, or to take full responsibility for one's actions. Fear generates feelings of inadequacy, worthlessness, even wickedness. Fear sometimes takes the form of overaggressiveness and hostility, or of self-abasement and self-deceit. Fear is the basis of compulsive 'good luck' rituals, of extreme shyness, of withdrawal from human companionship, of extreme self-love, of alcoholism and of narcotic addiction. Fear is the basis of all hatreds.

"Psychiatry can often bring these hidden fears into the open so that they can be recognized as the evil things they are. But to recognize them is not enough. Cure depends upon replacement of those fears with something else—faith, hope, sympathy and understanding for others—love.

"I advise writers who come to me about their stories and scripts—and surprising numbers do come for such advice—to think of the human heart as a vessel that *must be kept filled*. It does little good for psychiatry or medicine to empty the heart of its fears unless they are replaced with love and its attributes. Remember, a man's heart will be filled whether or no. It cannot remain empty, nor can it remain partially filled. If emptied of fears that are not replaced by love, understanding and faith, the heart will promptly refill itself with other fears and anxieties.

"Remember, too, that no man can *will* good into his heart, nor can a man *will* himself to love. All good emotions are spiritual. It is through prayer that good comes to man. Near my desk, if I were a writer, I'd hang the following quotation from Dr. Alexis Carrel, one of the great medical scientists:

> Only in prayer do we achieve that complete and harmonious assembly of body, mind and spirit which gives the frail human reed its unshakable strength.

"As an example of the inspiring type of story that will give your scripts spiritual significance, I've requested our guest Adele Eckbert to tell you how after all seemed hopeless, prayer brought her peace of mind and spirit. But first, let me urge you to not preach, nor force your religious convictions on viewers and readers. The surest way to cause viewers to lose interest in your play is to keep calling attention to the lesson he's already learned—*if* your story was properly written. If your script requires explaining, you've botched the job. And eschew, once for all, the misconception that viewers are morons who must be 'written down to.' Your story will have been successful if some reader or viewer in time of stress or need recalls the lesson it taught, and thereby is helped."

Mrs. Eckbert was a pleasant-voiced widow of about thirty-five. When she stood to speak to us she appeared to be a woman without a care. She said:

"Until my husband's accidental death four years ago,

I worked as his helper in the small toy factory he operated in two rooms of our home. Insurance money was barely enough to cover household expenses, so I continued operating the factory myself. I abandoned manufacture of some items because they required mechanical ability beyond mine. But the more simple toys —particularly those made with wooden blocks, beads and disks—kept me busy from morning until night. Ours was not a high-profit line; consequently, there was seldom money to spend on luxuries.

"Saturdays and holidays, our seven-year-old daughter Irma worked beside me, helping assemble some of the more colorful toys. She was a happy, ingenious child, and we became very close. It was a truly lovely association, one that I hoped we could maintain at least until Irma married and had a home of her own.

"One day after I'd been operating the factory for six months, I took Irma with me to Bellevue Hospital to visit a neighbor's child who'd been stricken with polio. The little girl seemed to be making a good recovery, and on my way from the hospital I stopped at the office to say a word of thanks.

"Six weeks later, Irma awakened one morning, complaining of a stiff neck. She was slightly feverish, so I kept her in bed and treated her for a cold. That night she complained of difficulty in moving her legs. I called a doctor, who promptly carried her to his car, took her to Bellevue and installed her in the children's polio ward.

"Irma's smile as she bade me good-by in the hospital stayed with me all during a wakeful night. As I paced the floor, frightened and heartsick, I kept asking, 'How could this happen to us—to Irma—sweet, generous, warmhearted. Why has this happened?' Toward morning, I got what I believed was the answer—Irma had contracted polio when we'd gone to visit her little play-mate.

"Suddenly I was overwhelmed with an intense fear of hospitals, and everything connected with them—doctors, nurses, orderlies, even visitors. In my mind, I pictured hospitals filled with unseen clouds of germs, microbes and viruses. I imagined them swarming on doctors' clothing and hands.

"Gentlemen," Mrs. Eckbert said, "my fear grew and grew, although I *knew* that hospitals were probably more free of contagion than other communities. I stopped shaking hands with friends because they might contaminate me. I began staying away from crowds, stopped riding in the subway, attended no meetings, and walked blocks to avoid passing close to hospitals.

"Worst of all, I soon found myself unable to enter the toy factory because of germs I imagined had been brought in with manufacturing materials. I began selling my small surplus toy stock, knowing that when it was all gone I'd be without income of any kind. I grew haggard.

"At the hospital, Irma had been supplied with braces for her legs, and word was sent to me that she was ready to come home. However, when I went to get her, the doctors noted my nervous condition and told me that until my health improved, Irma should remain in the polio ward.

"The next morning I made an appointment to visit Dr. Overmeyer. After greeting me, he motioned me to a chair, seated himself near by and said:

" 'Begin at the beginning, Mrs. Eckbert.'

" 'Doctor,' I said, 'I've come to lay my troubles in your lap—all of them. I can't carry them any longer.'

" 'And do you think that by laying your problems in my lap you'll be rid of them, Mrs. Eckbert?' he asked.

" 'I hope so. That's what psychiatrists are for, isn't it, Doctor?'

" 'Not exactly,' he said. 'But go ahead and tell me everything you care to. I'm a good listener.'

"So I started with Irma's polio attack, and told of the development of my fears, my growing dread of crowds, and finally, of the near-panic that overwhelmed me at the very thought of entering the toy factory workroom.

Dr. Overmeyer then asked me to tell him something of my background. When I had finished, he said:

" 'And now that you've given me a brief summary of recent emotional disturbances, what do you expect me to do, Mrs. Eckbert?'

" 'I expect you to treat my illness scientifically, of course. I've read many magazine and newspaper articles about psychology and psychoanalysis, Doctor.'

" 'Yes. But such articles,' Dr. Overmeyer said disapprovingly, 'mislead readers. Psychology is *not* a science, Mrs. Eckbert. Our knowledge of the mind is extremely rudimentary, and psychology is so complicated that I doubt that it will ever be a science.'

" 'You dismay me, Doctor,' I said. 'I don't quite know what to say. I thought psychologists agreed that . . .'

" 'Psychologists seldom agree on anything, Mrs. Eckbert. We can't even agree on what is humanity's basic drive. One group says it's self-gratification. A second school thinks it's the will-to-power. A third group believes our basic drive is a search for security. Many think our drive is escape from frustrations. A growing group thinks our drive is toward a search for God. Personally, I'm of the school of Dr. Viktor Frankl, president of the Austrian Society of Medical Psychotherapy, who teaches that humanity's great emotional problems are due to spiritual repression.'

" 'Are you trying to tell me that you can't help me, Dr. Overmeyer?' I asked.

" 'Psychiatry,' he said, 'can reveal hidden motives, and when such motives are understood by a patient, he can, if he has the will power, set himself on a course that will result in cure. You'll notice, Mrs. Eckbert, that I said "if he has the will power." Unfortunately, millions of persons are emotionally distressed or ill because they lack will power. Instead of psychoanalysis, these millions need the therapy of prayer.'

" 'But modern thinking, Doctor,' I began.

" 'Much of what is called modern thinking is atheistic thinking, and it has led us down a dark road. Despite psychiatry, our mental hospital population grows because psychiatry has ignored the spiritual side of man. Spirituality and morality are essence, and they can be acquired only through faith—never from books and articles. Faith comes through prayer, and those who pray truly need never visit a psychiatrist.'

" 'Am I to understand,' I asked, 'that you don't believe in psychology? Or, should I say, "psychiatry"?'

" 'To understand my viewpoint, you must know, Mrs. Eckbert, that in Germany as a young practicing psychoanalyst, I believed what I'd been taught—that only the unsophisticated discussed God and religion. I believed that humans were driven chiefly by sex, will-to-power and an assortment of lesser motivations. I had faith in Freudian analysis—permitting the patient to dredge to the surface all the doubts, fears, guilt feelings, memories of sins and soul-destroying emotions that had been buried in the subconscious mind. I believed that when those things were brought into the light, the patient would be freed of their ill effects.

" 'One day I was abruptly thrown into the Dachau concentration camp, a place of horrors. In the barracks where I was confined were hundreds of unfortunates, many of whom—unable to stand the torment—had become insane. As a psychiatrist there was nothing I could do for that group, but I tried to help those who still retained their sanity. My hard-won techniques were of no avail—I was able to help none.

" 'Through the prisoners' underground, I began getting reports of another barracks in which many prisoners had mysteriously adapted to distress and suffering—some to such a degree that they were able to find a measure of happiness in that man-made hell. This report seemed incredible, and for weeks I considered it a prison-bred fantasy. Then I learned that Dr. Viktor Frankl, a psychiatrist of repute, was telling each prisoner that if he were to remain sane, he *must forget himself entirely*, and devote all his mental, physical and spiritual energies to helping others.

" 'I knew, of course, that all neurotics are too self-centered, and saw the reasonableness of Frankl's advice, but it was the word "spiritual" that caused me to pause. If a man like Frankl believed in spirituality, perhaps the inclusion of God and religion in the practice of psychiatry wasn't so unsophisticated after all.

" 'In time, I learned that if man's spiritual side is permitted full expression all will be well with his mental, emotional and physical factors. I began teaching this to my fellow prisoners, and so it was that insanity among them dropped to almost zero.

" 'Incidentally, Dr. Frankl, who, while a prisoner, gave himself completely to the welfare of others, survived three concentration camps and came back to the world to found a psychological school of thought based on Christian concepts.

" 'I learned during those dark days that man, of himself, cannot nurture or develop his spiritual nature, but that it can be made to burgeon through the simple process of prayer. And I now teach that prayer opens the doorway to God, and that once that door is open, our fears, hatreds, anxieties, worries and physical illnesses become as if they never were. And that's why, Mrs. Eckbert, as your psychiatrist, I now advise you to go home and pray.'

" 'You consider me a weakling, don't you, Doctor?' I said.

" 'None of us—none of the fifty *million* who are crying out today for some sort of psychiatric treatment—was born a weakling, Mrs. Eckbert. At birth we're endowed with will power sufficient for our needs. In those of us who've exercised it by determinedly attacking each problem as it came up, will power remained vigorous. In those of us who followed the "easier" paths, will power became feeble. Our paths were made too easy because, among other things, parents made too many decisions for us that we should have been permitted to make for ourselves; because in high school we were permitted to take the least arduous courses; because in college we dropped difficult subjects in favor of more pleasant ones; because we formed the habit of permitting, or asking, others—family, friends, teachers, husbands, wives, ministers, psychologists, writers, lecturers, radio and television pitchmen, advertising blurbists, politicians—to decide what we should do and think. Finally, when a day came on which we had to face a difficult decision alone, we attempted to evade the responsibility by developing psychologically induced fears, or tremors, or pains, or any of a hundred other "symptoms" which we then took to a psychiatrist in the hope that he would turn us into robots.

" 'But will power is never entirely lost, Mrs. Eckbert, no matter how flabby we permit it to become. And when, with the help of prayer, we revive our will power, we can again face our problems with assurance that all will go well. Prayer, Mrs. Eckbert, is the only *perfect* psychotherapy. Jeremy Taylor, famed English bishop and author, wrote of it':

> Prayer is the peace of our spirit, the stillness of our thoughts, the evenness of our recollection, the seat of meditation, the rest of our cares, and the calm of our tempest.

"I felt a vague sense of serenity as Dr. Overmeyer quoted Taylor, but I made no comment. After glancing at me momentarily, he went on:

" 'In addition to being a great physician, Alexis Carrel was versed in psychology. He wrote':

> Prayer, like radium, is a luminous and self-generating form of energy.

" 'Well, Doctor,' I said, rising to leave, 'you may be right; I wouldn't know.'

" 'Spirituality as an element in psychology is being accepted more and more,' he continued. 'In fact, we now have psychiatrists and religious leaders working together in a National Academy of Religion and Mental Health.' He opened the door for me and said: 'Goodby, Mrs. Eckbert. I hope I've helped you.'

" 'I'll have to think things over,' I said. 'You've surprised me—I was expecting something different.'

"He smiled. 'I know,' he said.

"I was so perplexed—even irritated—by the way my interview with Dr. Overmeyer had turned out that I was home before I realized I'd mingled with Fortieth Street crowds, and had pushed my way into a jam-packed subway train without even thinking of my dread of close contacts. I was annoyed by Dr. Overmeyer because, among other things, I felt he'd been too brusque. I'd gone to him hoping for psychiatric help, and instead had received what amounted to a sermon. It seemed to me that the doctor had stepped out of his field; if I'd wanted spiritual help, I told myself, I'd have gone to a minister in the first place.

"As I went about household tasks, I grew more and more perturbed over the doctor's assumption that I was unable to make decisions for myself. But as I looked back over my life I was forced to admit that I'd chosen the easier, more pleasant way in almost every undertaking. I also had to admit that most of my decisions had been made for me by others. My parents had never treated me as a responsible individual. They'd never permitted me to share in the work of the home, to make my own toys, or to choose the clothes I'd wear to school or to parties.

"Mother didn't like me to straighten up my room, make my bed or hang things in my closet 'because you make such a mess.' On the few occasions when I did those things anyway, Mother'd do everything over.

"One afternoon—I was seven or eight—while Mother was at a neighbor's, I got the idea I could bake a wonderful cake. I went to the kitchen, got a large bowl, half filled it with icebox leftovers—carrots, tomatoes, mashed potatoes, a baked apple and pieces of meat. I salted and peppered the mixture generously, added a cup or two of sugar and a sifter of flour. I stirred lustily with a wooden spoon, then put the mess into the oven and turned on the heat. I remembered I'd forgotten to use baking powder, so I opened the oven door, reached in and emptied the almost full can of it on top of my 'cake.' I closed the oven door gently so the cake wouldn't fall, then went to the front porch to wait for Mother so I'd lose no time in showing her my masterpiece.

"I'll never forget my consternation when I skipped

ahead of Mother into a smoke-filled kitchen, nor my horror when she jerked open the oven door, grabbed a towel and tossed my cake—bowl and all—through an open kitchen window. Nor will I forget my humiliation when after one disgusted look at me, without speaking a word, she went about the business of cleaning up the mess I'd made.

"I tried once or twice to tell Mother I was sorry, but the words wouldn't come. I spent two miserable days waiting for her to give me an opportunity to explain that the cake would have been a glorious one if it hadn't burned, but Mother never mentioned the incident, and it wasn't long before my dreams of being a cakemaker turned to dismay at the mere thought of cooking—a dismay that stayed with me until long after I had married.

"I recalled that as a child if I was slow in putting on my shoes, Mother would impatiently lace and tie them for me; that I was seldom permitted to strap my books to carry to school 'because you make the strap so tight it crimps the edges of the covers.' I recalled that Father did much of my homework for me—particularly arithmetic—which I never did fully grasp. In other words, I began to realize that Mother and Father had failed to help me to develop into an independent youngster.

"For nine days following my interview with Dr. Overmeyer I stayed home, not even visiting Irma in the hospital, and during that time my fears were in evidence only when I thought of the toy factory. Once when I determinedly put my hand on the doorknob to enter, I began to tremble so violently that I feared I would fall. It was hours before I grew calm.

"My resentment at the things Dr. Overmeyer had said to me continued to grow, yet I had to admit that he'd caused me to look at myself with new eyes. I had reviewed my early life many times, of course, but always with a certain smugness because I'd been a pampered child. Now I began to think that if my parents had loved me more wisely, they'd have given me more opportunities to develop individuality. It had been Father who had encouraged me to take the easier courses in high school. I recalled him saying: 'Life's dreary enough, Adele, without making it drearier by cramming and drudging. In high school these days there are lots of pleasant courses for which you can earn credits. I don't think that *what* you study is so important, but what *is* important is to get that college degree. You'd like to be a schoolteacher. Well, with a degree, you can get a teaching job even if you're mediocre. Without a degree, you couldn't teach even if you were the best teacher in the state.'

"I hadn't been long in high school until I learned that the majority of my fellow students felt the same way. Consequently, we passed up difficult academic courses when we could. And that's the way it had been through college, too. There, I'd belonged to a group of students who would have been humiliated if they'd earned a better than C grade. We looked on those with B and B-plus averages as plebeians.

"A month after I'd graduated from college, Father died, and I felt terribly lost. Then I had married Hermann Eckbert—an unexciting, but solid, forceful person with whom I felt safe and secure.

"On the morning of the tenth day after my visit with Dr. Overmeyer, I needed something from the toy factory, hurriedly opened the door, stepped inside and was immediately almost overcome with fear that amounted to terror. Half hysterical, I went into the dining room and called Dr. Overmeyer on the telephone. Trying to keep panic out of my voice, I said:

" 'I'm coming to see you, Doctor, right away. You've just *got* to help me.'

" 'Something happen?' he asked.

" 'I went into the factory, and suddenly it seemed filled with evil presences—germs, maybe. Anyway, my heart began racing until I thought I'd choke. When it slowed, I got cold and weak. You *must* help me, Doctor.'

" 'And prayer didn't help?'

" 'Doctor,' I said desperately, 'don't torture me. You know I don't believe in prayer. Anyway, I've forgotten *how* to pray.'

" 'No one forgets how to pray, Mrs. Eckbert,' he said. 'In fact, no one can help praying when there seems no other way in which to turn. Kneel and ask God to show you why you become terrified when you enter the toy factory. Actually, Mrs. Eckberg, you know the reason, but you won't admit it in your conscious mind. And I could tell you the reason, but it wouldn't help, for you wouldn't believe me. I'll give you a hint, however. Wasn't your mother confined to a wheel chair for some time before she died?'

" 'She'd been crippled in an accident. I told you all about that. But *please*, Doctor, please help me.'

" 'To be cured,' he said, 'you must get at the truth for yourself.' I didn't answer. He quoted gently: 'And the truth shall make you free, Mrs. Eckbert,' and hung up.

"I was still sitting beside the telephone wringing my hands when my banker called to tell me that a retailer to whom I'd sold toys had gone broke; that the bill of sale the bank had discounted was unpaid, and that the bank wanted my check for eight hundred and forty dollars by return mail. Dazedly I opened my bankbook and saw I had less than one thousand dollars left. That meant I'd have to sell more toys from reserve stock— which meant that I'd have to enter the factory no matter how terrifying it might be.

"I was numb with worry, when a few minutes later, I

opened the door to a social worker who told me that Irma had become uncooperative, and was pleading to come home. 'She'll arrive by ambulance late this afternoon,' the woman said, and went on her way.

"Life had suddenly become too much for me. Trapped, helpless, alone and desperate, I sank to my knees, and heard my voice saying:

" 'Help me, God. Oh, please help me.'

"Crying softly, I then went to the bedroom, lay face down on the bed, and for a long time I remained there without thought and without feeling, I fell asleep at last, and when I awakened, I *knew* what had caused my fears; knew why I dreaded entering the factory; knew why I'd refused to pray—until forced to my knees. And I felt as I sat on the edge of the bed that a clean wind had swept through my mind as I had lain there, carrying away with it self-delusions, self-complacency, self-love and my false sense of self-sufficiency. I saw myself as I'd really been—and I was ashamed.

"Ashamed, yes. But also, my soul was warm with a new, deep silence. As I changed the sheets on Irma's bed, put flowers in a vase on her bedside table and replaced the somewhat drab window curtains with some brightly figured cretonne, it seemed to me that the thundering of a cataract within me had suddenly ceased, and that in the strange new silence I could hear soundless music. I didn't try to understand what had happened during the short time I'd 'slept.' I only knew it had been an answer to my soul's cry to God for help—a cry torn from my despair—a cry that must have revealed to Heaven that I was aware at last that without God, I was nothing.

"I felt so puzzled as to why God would answer the prayer of one who had long thought of prayer as salve for the superstitious that I telephoned Dr. Overmeyer to see if he could supply the answer. His office girl said he was busy, but that she'd have him phone when he was free. I wanted also to tell him that my fears had vanished, but I first wanted to be certain that they had, so rather nervously, I walked to the door of the toy factory, put my hand on the knob, breathed a silent prayer for strength and walked into the workshop. It was redolent with the clean odors of sawdust and shavings, and the tools racked above the benches seemed to invite me to use them. I felt an eagerness to get back to work.

"As I stood there realizing that because fear had vanished, I could work again, tears of happiness filmed my eyes. Impulsively I knelt and said, "Thank you, God.'

"Mrs. Glover, the social worker, had said Irma would arrive home late in the afternoon, which meant that there were still a couple of hours to wait. I went into Irma's room and just sat there, marveling at the mysterious power of prayer. Less than two hours ago—my agonized prayer echoing in my heart—I'd thrown myself across my bed. And I'd slept. Not for long, perhaps half an hour. Yet I'd awakened with an assurance that I was protected and sheltered, and as completely aware of the causes of my emotional illnesses as if I'd undergone the most prolonged psychoanalysis.

"As a result of my prayer, I realized that deep within me had been a fear of cripples—a fear probably born of the unhappy days and nights with my accident-crippled mother. And I realized the shocking truth that my unconscious mind had developed a determination not to permit a crippled Irma to come home. My conscious mind, of course, would have rejected such a thought with horror; so my subconscious had gone to work developing fears that tended to make Irma's return impossible.

"The shame of this discovery had seemed almost too much to bear until I realized that it was not Irma, my daughter, I'd been rejecting, but her crippled condition.

"Knowing nothing in my conscious mind of the evil broth being brewed in my subconscious, it was no wonder that my emotional, physical and mental life had become confusion confounded.

"The phone rang. It was Dr. Overmeyer, and I told him what had happened to me, explaining the birth and growth of my fears in almost the same words I've just said to you.

"He chuckled, and said: "The way you've expressed your conclusions, Mrs. Eckbert, would throw some of the more pedantic psychoanalysts into a dither. But scientific jargon or not, you've related exactly what happened. How do you feel now, about Irma coming home?'

" 'My heart is filled with love,' I said, 'and I know that God will show me how to help, Doctor. I'm sure, very sure.'

"We talked a few minutes longer, then suddenly Irma was home—in a wheel chair. Mrs. Glover helped me put her into bed, with Suzie, her favorite doll, cuddled in her arms. She quickly fell asleep, and in order not to disturb her, we went to another room to talk. The social worker said:

" 'Irma refuses to use her legs, refuses even to attempt to walk in her new braces. Something's bothering her—some fear or worry. We don't know what, because she won't talk about it. You, Mrs. Eckbert, must get to the root of her lack of co-operation. Remember that if Irma will co-operate, with proper exercise and practice, she'll walk again.'

"Now, Gentlemen," Mrs. Eckbert said as she paused to drink a glass of water, "before I tell you how God, through prayer, not only enabled Irma to walk again, but so guided me in my toy manufacturing that finances need never again be a problem, I want to explain as best

I can what I've discovered about prayer during the four years that have passed since Irma contracted polio.

"Although I've learned a great deal from Dr. Over-meyer, and from ministers and others, my greatest help toward understanding came from reading the New Testament, where to my surprise I found that Jesus discussed prayer on seventy-three different occasions, and that twenty-two of Jesus' own prayers are recorded. I don't believe that even the most skeptical can read Jesus' teachings concerning prayer and remain in doubt. Jesus not only commanded us to pray, but He told us how to pray. Five times He gave us Divine directions for prayer. He referred to different kinds of prayer, and He told us to whom prayers should be addressed. He told of the benefits to be derived from prayer, and of Divine promises connected with prayer. And He even gave examples of wrong kinds of prayer.

"Jesus' own prayers, as recorded in the four Gospels, were for God's recognition, for strength to endure enmity, for wisdom. He prayed to thank God for food, for gifts and favors, for children, for relief in distress, to know God's will, for believers, for the apostles, for blessing on the Bread, for God's glory, and He prayed as private devotion. He gave us the Lord's Prayer, and conducted prayers with others. On the Cross, He prayed God to forgive His persecutors, and for the return of His vision of God.

"And now, Gentlemen, I'll sum up briefly what I now know to be true about prayer. I say 'know to be true' because prayer has worked out so beautifully in my life. This is my belief:

"I believe that the answers to our true prayers have been part of God's universe since the beginning of time. I believe the answers exist, and have always existed. I believe that prayer is a channel through which God's answers flow to us. I believe that we obstruct this channel by selfishness, in any of its innumerable forms. I believe that our channel to God will remain open to God's bounties as long as we maintain a willingness to do His will in all things. I believe that the soul of the lowliest peasant is as important to God as the soul of the greatest prelate, and that prayer answers are for all—the high and the low—when we pray, not for what *we* want, but for what God knows is best for us. I believe that faith is a spiritual element that grows with exercise; that even though faith be small at first, it will, through use, grow to become the key to all the good things of life."

"During the morning of Irma's second day at home," Mrs. Eckbert told us, "a visiting nurse from the hospital instructed me on how to massage Irma's leg muscles while Irma was in her bath. 'Irma's fortunate,' the nurse said, 'that her left leg requires only exercise and massage to become perfectly well. Her right leg's not in such good condition; treatment of it will probably be prolonged. However, in time that leg, too, should respond fully. Let her begin by taking one step each day while you support her weight by holding her under the arms from behind. Persistence is what counts.'

"I left Irma in the tub, her doll within reach, when I'd gone to show the nurse out. When I returned to the bathroom, Irma was holding Suzie's legs under water and was vigorously massaging them. I took the doll from her and while drying it with a towel, said:

" 'That wasn't a good way to treat an expensive doll, Irma. Pull the plug now, and when the water's all drained out, I'll dry you right there. And then, dear, we'll try taking your first step. Aren't you thrilled—your first step!'

"She didn't answer, and when I glanced at her, she was silently crying.

" 'Why, darling,' I said, 'did you think I was angry?'

"She still didn't answer, so I knelt beside the tub and started to put my arms around her. She pulled away.

" 'Now, dear,' I said, 'we must get you out of the tub. And while I hold you, you can try moving your legs—try taking one little teeny step.'

" 'No,' she said.

" 'But Irma . . .'

" 'Please put my braces on, Mother, and put me in bed,' she said.

" 'But Irma, darling. Don't you want to try to walk?'

" 'No,' she said sullenly, then hesitated and mumbled: 'No, thank you.'

"I tried to not show how disturbed I was as I wrapped a fresh, dry towel around her, carried her to her bed, put her braces back on and tucked her snugly between the sheets. Her sullen expression hadn't changed.

" 'Well, darling,' I said, 'you're back in bed—just as you wanted. Is there anything I can get you, anything you'd especially like?'

" 'Suzie,' she said.

" 'Of course,' I said, and went to the bathroom, got Suzie and handed her to Irma. 'Shall I get a fresh dress for Suzie, dear?' I asked.

" 'No, thank you,' Irma answered. She hugged the naked doll to her, turning her back to me. I stood for a few moments, biting my lower lip uncertainly, unable to fathom this strange mood. Then I patted her shoulder and went into the factory to try to finish assembling an order for manikins made from colored wooden beads.

"I didn't work long, however, for sullen resentment in Irma was something I'd never seen before. Recalling that the social worker who had brought Irma home had said she's been unco-operative in the hospital, I went to the telephone, called the hospital and asked to speak to someone familiar with Irma's case. After a long wait, one of the polio ward nurses answered. I told her about Irma's attitude, and her refusal to walk. The nurse said:

" 'That's the way she reacted here, Mrs. Eckbert, whenever we tried to get her to exercise her legs. Something's troubling Irma. Try to discover what it is. However, if her attitude doesn't change in ten days or two weeks, perhaps she'd better come back here and let our psychologists see what they can find out. Please call us and report progress.'

"During the next six days, Irma was a cheerful, talkative, co-operative little girl except when I'd suggest that she try to walk. Then, with eyes flashing resentfully, she'd hug Suzie to her and retire into stubborn silence. During those six days I was patient and forbearing, but on the seventh day I decided to try sternness. That was a mistake, for Irma turned pale and became nauseated. I put her to bed, noticed her forehead was beaded with sweat, felt it and found it cold as ice. Frightened, I called Dr. Overmeyer. He was out of town, and when I hung up the receiver, the fears returned, the ones I thought I'd lost forever. I began wringing my hands.

"By an effort of will, I calmed my mounting panic and forced myself to *think*. Once again I was faced with the responsibility of making a decision for myself. Should I take Irma back to the hospital? Should I wait for Dr. Overmeyer's return? Should I face this crisis alone? Alone! I *wasn't* alone—God was with me—in my heart—all around me. I felt an immediate and wonderful release from tension. I knelt by my chair and prayed:

" 'God, help me to make my decision, and give me the will power to carry that decision through. With Your help, I accept responsibility. I'll act as You want me to act, Father.'

"Certain that God would direct me, I got to my feet, went into the factory and calmly finished the job I'd been working on. Then I went into Irma's bedroom, saw she was awake, gently took Suzie from her arms, and said:

" 'I wonder what Suzie thinks about your refusing to exercise your legs? I'm sure if Suzie were in your place, she'd try very hard to get completely well.'

"With a little cry, Irma held out her arms to me. I bent close and took her into my own. She pressed her face to mine, and with tears running down her face sobbed:

" 'I was doing it for Suzie, Mother, because nobody likes Suzie.'

" 'What makes you think that, Irma? I'm sure everyone likes Suzie—I love her very much. Where in the world did you get the idea that Suzie isn't liked?'

" 'They made braces for me and all of the kids, but they didn't make braces for Suzie.' She choked up with sobs. I comforted her, my mind racing. Was this God's answer? Of course it was! I wept with Irma, but with joy. After a while, I asked:

" 'If Suzie had braces just like yours, would you try to teach her to walk, Irma?'

" 'Oh, yes, Mother, I would! I would!'

" 'But dear,' I said, thinking quickly, 'Suzie couldn't learn to walk by herself. You'll have to teach her, show her how. You'd have to set her a good example by trying hard yourself—every day. Would you do that?'

" 'Of course, Mother. She's only a doll. I'll have to help her just like you'll help me. Can she have braces, Mother? Can she? Oh, please, can she?'

"Gentlemen, my discovery of the frustration that was the cause of Irma's refusal to try to walk was an immediate answer to prayer. It could have been nothing else, for Irma didn't even wait for Suzie's braces to be finished before beginning her own exercise—wanting, she said, to be sure she could teach Suzie properly. And two years later, Irma and Suzie together, discarded their braces forever. Today, Irma walks as well as I, and she smiles as she says:

" 'I knew all the time, Mother, that I was just playing a game with Suzie. But Mother, it was a very important game.'

"Not long after Irma began taking exercises, the wholesaler who bought most of my toys came to tell me that the demand for most old-fashioned toys had decreased; that today's youngsters wanted more modern playthings. He suggested I experiment with what he called 'space-age gadgets.' I prayed about this decision, too—asking God to guide me. Today my little factory's busy—not making modern toys, but toys that actually help crippled children. For instance:

"A neighbor's child, not yet four years old, came home from the hospital in need of special leg exercises —just as Irma had done. One day her doctor said to me:

" 'Climbing up steps is the finest exercise this little girl could have, but she's too small to climb standard steps. If you'd make some steps shallow enough for a child to climb . . .' His voice died and he looked inquiringly at me.

" 'I'll do my best, Doctor,' I said. Then I went to work, and after several days came up with a set of two wide, shallow steps that led up to a thirty-inch square platform, with two other steps descending on the opposite side.

"The child's doctor was delighted. He persuaded me to paint the steps in bright colors, and to add a sturdy railing to help the little girl climb and to keep her from falling. I did those things, and the little girl loved her steps. She's spent many happy hours toddling up and down her pretty stairway. You who have visited department stores recently may have seen 'The Eckbert Magic Stile' on sale. They're selling well, for all toddlers delight in them.

"Other toys, some designed basically for handicapped youngsters, others distincly educational, are on the fire in my now somewhat expanded factory. All will be successful, for each is designed with the help of prayer. And should some of them not make much money that's all right, too, for my one desire for the toys is that they help those who need them.

"That, Gentlemen, is my prayer story. Good luck with your writing. May God bless it."

MY OCEANSIDE HOME in the northwestern tip of California is exactly halfway between Portland, Oregon and San Francisco, nine hours by car from either city. Thus, it's a convenient stopover place for friends driving in either direction, and we are seldom without guests.

The night I finished writing the following story about Elias Letwaba, three visitors arrived to spend the night— Robert Schlick, poet-writer (see "God's Ranch in Pleasant Valley"); Frank P. Robinson, fictioneer and writer on psychological subjects; and Kenneth Sanger, a stranger to me, who accompanied Robinson. Following a camp-style supper of baked beans, freshly caught ocean perch and fried potatoes, the conversation as it frequently does in my home, turned to the subject of prayer. Pointing to my typewriter, I said:

"That sheet of paper in the typewriter is the last page of a most unusual answer-to-prayer story, the story of one of Africa's most successful missionaries—a native."

"You know, Lake," Sanger said, "I've read your book Your Prayers are Always Answered, *and occasionally, I run across one of your prayer stories in some magazine. Tell me—I don't mean to be offensive—do you really believe some of those fantastic answers to prayer that you report?"*

"Of course I do. Don't you?"

"Some I can believe," Sanger said, "but some I can't. You know, Lake, when you write about answers to prayer that violate natural laws, well—I can't believe that God goes around breaking His own rules for the universe. Some of the supposed miracles you write about are physically impossible."

"Are you a scientist?" I asked.

"Not exactly, but I'm intellectual, a reasoning man."

I went to my desk, got the "Letwaba" manuscript, handed it to Schlick, and said: "Read this to us, Bob. When you have finished, I want to ask Sanger some questions."

When Schlick had finished, I looked inquiringly at Sanger. He said:

"If you'd left out that part about the physical healings, I could go for the rest as psychological phenomena. But 'ten thousand sick permanently healed by prayer'—impossible—physically impossible."

Robinson motioned me to let him answer Sanger, so I sat back and listened.

"Are you familiar with the Second Law of Thermodynamics, Sanger?" Robinson asked.

"Is that the Law of Entropy?"

"Yes."

"Sorry, my education didn't include theoretical physics."

"Well, let me ask you this: Supposing some morning you went into the kitchen, put a kettle of cold water on the stove, turned on the heat, but instead of boiling, half the water in the kettle turned to ice. Would you consider that a physical impossibility?"

"Ridiculous," Sanger said.

"Well, then, let's say that on a day of average temperature, a man sitting on a chair in an ordinary room suddenly fell to the floor and died of suffocation because the countless billions of air molecules that had been evenly distributed throughout the room a moment before had accumulated in half the room, leaving the half in which the man had been sitting absolutely without air. Is that a physical impossibility?"

"You know it is, Frank."

"Okay. Now try your intellect on this one: Suppose

you were watching a glass of water standing on a table, and suddenly the upper half of the water shot toward the ceiling with the speed of a bullet, leaving the lower half of the water in the glass. Or suppose you're watching that same glass of water, and suddenly the upper half begins to boil violently while, at the same time, the lower half of the water turns to ice. Physically impossible, Sanger?"

"You're playing games, Frank—all your examples are physically impossible. They're against the laws of nature. What does all this rigmarole have to do with Lake's prayer answers?"

"This," Robinson said. "According to the Second Law of Thermodynamics, all four of those examples are possible, and are not violations of physical laws. If you doubt me, get in touch with one of the world's leading physicists George Gamow, professor of theoretical physics at George Washington University. And incidentally, those last three examples I gave you are Gamow's own illustrations of the workings of the Law of Entropy. So, me lad, now that your skepticism's been refuted by a man far more intellectual than yourself, do you feel—if you know nothing about theoretical physics— you should be spouting off about what is—or what isn't possible with God?"

Letwaba

SHORTLY AFTER MIDDAY ONE JUNE IN THE EARLY 1920's a middle-aged, black-bearded native preacher, dust covered and weary, a Bible under one arm, walked into a town about two hundred miles north of Pretoria in the

Transvaal, stepped onto a sidewalk and was promptly knocked down into a gutter by a passing white man.

"Stay in the street, Kaffir," the white man said, and walked away without a backward glance.

Nowhere in the world are blacks so shabbily treated as in South Africa, and nowhere in South Africa are they more mistreated than in some areas of the Transvaal.

Elias Letwaba, the preacher, was the son of a chief of the Ndebele tribe. He spoke three European and four native languages. He'd been an itinerant preacher for more than twenty-one years, and during those years he'd been stoned, beaten, starved, cursed, kicked and otherwise persecuted by both whites and blacks. Yet he worked on, meek, courageous, prayerful, following to the best of his ability in the footsteps of Jesus. He preached a simple message of Christian love that despite revilings and spiteful usage had enabled him to number his converts to Christ in the tens of thousands.

Now he arose from the gutter, picked up his Bible, tucked it again under an arm and proceeded down the center of the dusty street to the town square where he was met by a small group of white Christians who'd invited him to speak to them.

Letwaba took a position beside a large geranium bush that bore bright red blossoms, and began to deliver his talk. He'd spoken only a few minutes, however, when a white mob rushed him, hurled him to the ground, stoned and kicked him, shouting:

"Preach to white people, will you, you black devil! We'll teach you to preach to respectable whites!"

White women, who were among the group who had invited him, pushed their way through the angry mob, formed a protective circle around the fallen man and tongue-lashed the attackers until they fell back, glaring sullenly.

Letwaba regained his feet, wiped blood and dirt from his face and clothes, and speaking Dutch, he said to the members of the mob:

"My masters, when you send a letter by a little boy to another white man, does it matter if the boy be black or white? If he is black, does the man to whom the letter was sent rush the lad, beat him and tell him he had no right to bring the letter? Well, masters, I am only a little letter carrier—a nobody. I wouldn't presume to force my own opinions on you; I have come only to bring you a letter." He held up the Bible. "This letter. It is from One for whom you have great respect."

Then Letwaba began a simple gospel message, using no words of his own, but only quotes from the New Testament that were familiar to all present—investing Jesus' words with a richness, a fullness, and with such promise as the listeners had never heard before. Mumbled curses and threats died away as the audience heard God's message of love for the world and for them. They were being promised peace of heart, peace of mind, quietness of spirit, healthy bodies and the job of service to others.

Soon some were weeping, and Letwaba wept, too, for he saw that all—even the mobsters—had forgotten that it was a black man speaking. Later, one of the mob said:

"I was awed, because the words I heard seemed to be spoken by God Himself."

Years later, that town was to honor Letwaba as it had never honored any other man—black or white. Townspeople, almost to a man, were to voice respect, admiration and love for the man they'd once beaten and reviled.

When Elias Letwaba was nearing fourteen, he was given three books by a white man for whom he'd worked briefly as an oxen lead boy. The books, printed in Dutch—a language Letwaba had learned in childhood along with his own Ndebele dialect—were historical accounts of the lives of Lobengula, greatest of the Matabele kings; and of Chaka, mighty Zulu, the cruelest and most brilliant military leader Africa had ever known, and a dog-eared copy of the New Testament.

Young Letwaba, reading his books in the fields as he herded cattle, became a hero-worshiper—not of Lobengula, nor of Chaka—but of Jesus. While other boys of the tribe emulated the warlike characteristics of conquering chieftains, Letwaba, his heart warm with growing knowledge of a God of love, attempted to organize games in which kindness triumphed over cruelty. His efforts were met with scorn, and finally, with beatings.

"Not once," he told me in Johannesburg years later, "did the persecution of my playfellows anger me. Instead, I felt deep compassion for them. This made me happy, for I wanted Jesus' approbation more than anything in the world."

Soon after his fourteenth birthday, Letwaba, like other youths of his age, was scheduled to undergo tribal puberty rites. Much pain was involved, but Letwaba was not afraid of pain. He felt, however, that the vicious knowledge conveyed to the boys during the rites was wrong. So, with his father's permission, he refused initiation and became almost a pariah.

For several months, Letwaba was a bewildered boy. He couldn't understand how his fellows could prefer the savagery of warriors to the peace of spirit offered by Jesus. "I learned later," Letwaba told me, "that many of the boys would have liked to have heard more about Jesus, but feared evil spells from witch doctors who wanted no part of Christianity."

Young Letwaba prayed for guidance. A few days

after his prayer, the dry season ended, and the river near the kraal that had dwindled to a series of occasional shallow pools, became a thundering, yellow torrent, carrying on its raging crest the carcasses of cattle, antelope, sheep, and the trunks of uprooted trees.

When the flood was at its height, Letwaba, while eating from a cast-iron pot before his father's house, felt an overwhelming urge to walk down to the river's edge. He arrived there just as an old man, supporting himself with a crooked stick, started to cross the river at what had been a well-used ford. However, the ford had been washed out, and the old man was swept away. Instantly, Letwaba dived to the old fellow's rescue, and succeed in dragging him, unconscious, to a sandy shelf where he laid the man face down and pressed the water from his lungs.

When consciousness returned, the old man got to his feet, and trembling with weakness and emotion, took Letwaba's hands, and said:

"Thank you, little boy. God certainly sent you to rescue me."

"It was then," Letwaba told me, "that I knew God had destined me to rescue many souls—that He had chosen me to be a blessing to my fellows."

During the next five years, Letwaba studied industriously to the end that he would be able to explain God's Word with insight and intelligence. And in order that he could reach more people, he mastered German, Dutch, English, Tonga, Zulu, Xosa, and Suto. He was barely nineteen when, accompanied by his twelve-year-old brother Wilfred, he set out to carry to the tribes of northern Transvaal, as much of the story of Jesus as he understood.

It wasn't difficult for Preacher Letwaba and Wilfred to follow Jesus' instructions to the Seventy—that they "carry neither purse, nor scrip, nor shoes"—for neither of them had ever had more than a few pennies at one time, and neither had ever worn shoes. And so it was that the Letwabas, barefoot, hungry and travel worn, came to a village ruled by a drunken chief, a scoundrelly witch doctor, and a gorilla-like bully known as The Rhino, who sometimes acted as the witch doctor's executioner.

As a matter of customary courtesy, Letwaba first called on the chief to ask permission to talk to his people. The chief called the witch doctor from a nearby hut, motioned to Letwaba, then lay back on the ground and began to snore. The witch doctor ordered Letwaba from the kraal.

As Letwaba and Wilfred neared the boundary of the village, a young man, running after them, shouted for them to wait. He greeted Letwaba, then said.

"You are a Jesus man."

"It is so," Letwaba answered. "How did you know?"

"I was behind a hut, and heard you talking to the chief. I would know more about your God—of whom I heard when I was a houseboy in Potgeiter's Rust."

"Let us rest while I talk," Letwaba said, and squatted on his haunches. The young man squatted also, and said:

"I am Manyao—called Tony by the whites. Speak now, my brother, and I will listen."

Letwaba then told the story of Jesus, of His love for mankind, of His promise of a quiet heart to those who would heed His teachings, of His death on the Cross.

"You have caused bright flowers to bloom in my breast," Manyao said.

"It is plain to me that the words that came to you from my mouth were put there by God," Letwaba said, "for you have heard them—and believe. Someday a greater teacher than I will come to your people. Remain in peace, O Manyao."

"Go safely, O-Man-of-the-Kind-God," Manyao said, and turned back toward the village.

Noting that Wilfred had fallen asleep in the grass, Letwaba walked to the river near by, sat on a boulder, stared wearily into the sluggishly flowing water and soon became interested in two large bull crocodiles that appeared suddenly out of the shadows on the opposite bank. The crocs swam toward each other, locked long-toothed jaws together and began a swirling, spashing, roaring battle.

In later years, Letwaba never talked much about the dangers and suffering he'd experienced during his years as a perambulating preacher. The most he would say when asked a point-blank question was some brevity such as: "In that kraal, they beat me . . ." "Near that village, I was stoned . . .""On that road a spear was hurled at me . . ." "In that valley a leopard attacked me . . ." "In that *kloof* a buffalo tossed my companión."

Of the episode that happened shortly after he and Wilfred had been expelled from the witch doctor's village, he'd relate only that some men had tried to kill him. It was Reverend Manyao Mabele—Letwaba's first convert—who gave me the following detailed account.

Seated on the rock beside the river, Letwaba had become so intent on the noisy battle of the two crocodiles that he failed to hear footsteps behind him, and it wasn't until a shadow fell across him that he turned to face a group of angry men led by a scowling, powerfully muscled, long-armed warrior.

For a few moments, no word was spoken. Then the scowling man said, "I am The Rhino. I am the servant of the witch doctor. I have come to kill you. Get to your feet."

"You will not kill me," Letwaba said.

"You must die, O Stranger. My master has said it." He pointed to the still-fighting crocodiles. "Our gods are there," he said. "They await your coming with hungry bellies."

"Those are not gods," Letwaba said, rising to his feet, "but monsters. My God is the One God—the God of Good—the All-Powerful. It comes to me that my God will not permit you to slay me, for I have work still to do for Him."

The Rhino laughed, lowered his head, stretched out his arms and leaped at Letwaba, who dropped to his knees in prayer. The Rhino, unable to check his rush, stumbled headlong over the kneeling man, crashed into the rock on which Letwaba had been sitting, got to his feet, staggered, then fell into the river.

The Rhino's followers stood transfixed as their leader sank beneath the water. The two crocodiles ceased their struggle and sank out of sight after him. Letwaba quickly waded into the river, ducked beneath the surface and came up holding The Rhino by a foot. He splashed his way to shore and dragged his enemy onto a mud flat a bare second before greedy jaws chomped hollowly within inches of The Rhino's head. The Rhino, still dazed from bumping his head on the boulder, sat up, looked at the crocodiles now fighting and bellowing again, observed the tracks made by his body when Letwaba had dragged him across the mud, and said:

"Your God knocked me into the river. Why, then, did you save me from the crocodiles?"

"Because my God loves you," Letwaba told him.

"What is love?"

"My God wants to be your friend. He knows that in your heart are much goodness and kindness. He also knows that in your heart is badness. He would take away the badness forever, and leave only the goodness."

"Your God is a wise God, for he knows what none other but I have known—that in my heart badness and goodness have long fought together as do yonder crocodiles. You have given me strange thoughts, O Rescuer. It comes to me that your God is stronger than my gods. I would call Him Master."

"That is good," Letwaba said, almost choked with emotion. "You may call Him Master, but to please Him, you must learn His ways. These I will teach you."

For two weeks, Letwaba and Wilfred lived in the brush near the village, explaining the New Testament to Manyao and The Rhino. Years later, Manyao became an ordained minister.

For the next nineteen years, Letwaba traveled the twisting, thorny trails of forest and veldt to hundreds of villages and kraals. Still barefoot, still penniless, he climbed rocky mountains, forded tumultuous rivers, waded through swamps and bogs, plodded across deserts and invaded forest jungles carrying his message of the God of Love. He spoke to crowds and to lone goatherds, to chieftains and to slaves, to headsmen and to sorcerers. In some villages, he was welcomed with shouts of joy; from others he was driven with blows and curses.

When stoned or beaten, he blessed his tormentors as he wiped away blood and dust. When discouragement rested heavily upon him, he'd walk far out on the open veldt, or climb to the top of some hill, and spend a night in prayer—asking God to let him continue to love those who persecuted him—for strength to resist self-aggrandizement—for assurance that his messages were of God, and not of himself.

At the end of those nineteen years, he numbered his converts by the thousands. Nevertheless, each year he'd grown more unhappy because of an increasing certainty that there was something vital missing from his ministry. When I interviewed him in Johannesburg, he explained it this way:

"After working for weeks with a group of new converts, explaining the New Testament, assuring them that they could take their problems to God in prayer with confidence that He'd help them, I'd leave them enthusiastic and apparently established in their new way of life only to return to that village a year later and find that many of them had reverted to the ways of the jungle. I knew, of course, that this 'backsliding'—as Americans call it—was common to the primitive congregations of all church denominations, but I'd prayed that those to whom I brought Jesus' teachings would remain steadfast in the Faith. That many didn't, made me feel guilty before God, because obviously I was leaving something vital out of my teaching."

African religious history is filled with cases of mass reversion, or backsliding. One such example is the French Cameroons where Africa's earliest missionaries converted the entire population, established churches and tribal congregations. Yet today, witchcraft is more pervasive there than it ever was, and pagan rites are now combined with perverted church ceremonies and rituals.

Such reversions are understandable to one who knows the primitive African mind. The ignorance of these primitives is abysmal. They have no idea of reality, possess no logic of things. To them, the sun is the sun and the moon is the moon; rain is rain and wind is wind. They cannot conceive of the sun as a burning star, nor of the moon as a reflector of sunlight. They know that rain is water, but do not know the why of the clouds. They have learned that death follows old age, that hunger is caused by lack of food. They know these things because they are familiar, but almost everything else that happens, they believe is caused by enchantment, evil spells or magic.

They know nothing of disease-carrying insects and germs, so when stricken with sleeping sickness or fever, there can be for them but one cause—the evil eye. If while hunting, they stumble and fall in front of some wild beast and are injured by it, they know that someone has cast an evil spell upon them—for haven't they hunted countless times before without stumbling?

For the infinitude of epidemics, disasters and famines that plague African tribesmen they know only one cure—counterspells cast by witch doctors. Except for a few things he's learned from tradition and has accepted as natural, to the primitive African everything is enchantment or magic—the good as well as the bad. The only person who can control this magic is the witch doctor. Consequently, he is the most powerful individual in tribal life—more powerful than the chief, except when, as is often the case, the chief is also a witch doctor.

"White missionaries," Letwaba said, "ignorant of these things, have sometimes caused confusion and needless suffering. I remember an instance where a newly arrived missionary urged his listeners to 'heap coals of fire on the heads of their enemies.' That night eighteen men were terribly burned when blazing coals were dumped on their heads while they slept.

"Great care must be used in translating the Bible for a tribesman. He is incapable of concepts of imagery, and must not be told that if his hand offend him he must cut if off, for he'll take it literally and appear some morning with a hand severed at the wrist.

"Now I, being a native, understood these things, and took them into account in my teaching. I did my best to bring God's message to my people with words and examples best suited to their understanding.

"I knew that God's words, when presented as He

wished them to be, assured that converts would remain faithful unto death. Therefore, because so many wavered and fell by the wayside, I reasoned that I was to blame—that my teachings did not inspire full spirituality. Something was missing from my messages. But What? I beseeched God for an answer, and while waiting for His revelation I read and reread the New Testament—searching for these things that, when understood, would sweep the jungle from the hearts of my listeners—sweep it away forever.

"Educators tell us that it requires three generations of civilization and education to remove the last traces of the jungle from primitives. This is true only when Christianity is not taken into account. I know native pseudo-Christian lawyers and doctors—graduates of English and French universities—who during the week wear European clothes, travel in the style befitting men of great knowledge, and on Sundays sit reverently in the pews of 'respectable' churches. Yet several times a year they may be found, armed with spears and naked, attending witchcraft rites deep in the forest. Despite their veneer of civilization, such men are still jungle men at heart. Education has done nothing for them spiritually.

"On the other hand, time and time again during these later years, I've seen God, through prayer, strip from the lives of such men their fear of evil spells, their superstitions, their dread of arousing enmity of witch doctors—cleanse them of the jungle heart—instantly and permanently.

"But to go back to my search for greater truths to give my people: I began making notes of certain Bible passages, and from their mass, the words 'heal' and 'healing' began to stand out. Such passages I listed in a separate notebook, and soon I had compiled a revealing series of memoranda such as:

"To the centurion who told Jesus that his servant was

home sick with the palsy, Jesus said: *I will come and heal him.* (Matt. 8:5-7)

And when he had called unto him his twelve disciples, he gave them power against unclean spirits, to cast them out, and to heal all manner of sickness and all manner of disease.
(Matt. 10:1)

"Acts 3 tells that when Peter and John saw a lame man lying at the gate of the temple, Peter said: '. . . *in the name of Jesus Christ of Nazareth rise up and walk.'* Then, verse 4 continues:

And he (Peter) took him by the right hand, and lifted him up, and immediately his feet and ankle bones received strength.

"Verse 8 tells how the man leaped, walked and praised God. And verse 9 says:

And all the people saw him walking and praising God.

"In Chapter 3 of I Peter, verse 4, Peter says, speaking of Jesus:

Who his own self bare our sins in his own body on the tree (cross), that we, being dead to sins, should live unto righteousness: by whose stripes we are healed.

"Away back in the time of Moses, God said to him: *I am the Lord that healeth thee.*

"There were more entries," Letwaba went on, "And

I prayed over them until I felt certain that God was still the healer of the body. It was a joyous revelation, and wishing to share it with others, I visited five white ministers of different church denominations. The first minister said:

" 'True, Letwaba, Jesus healed the sick when He was on earth, but when He died, the days of such miracles passed with Him.'

"The second minister said: 'It's blasphemous to ask God to heal the sick, for their diseases are sent by Him for their own good.'

"The third minister said: 'If God had meant that He would heal the sick if one prayed, the promise would have been for whites—not blacks.'

"The fourth minister said: 'I think God might still heal the sick if one had sufficient faith. But who in these days has such faith?'

"The fifth minister said: 'Does God heal the sick today? I wish I knew, Letwaba. I wish I knew.' "

The next phase of Letwaba's story was told to me by Manyao, who had now been Letwaba's companion and confidant for several years. He said:

"Following Letwaba's interviews with the five ministers, he came into our hut on the outskirts of town and sat silent and contemplative on a low stool. After what seemed to me a long time, he went to his knapsack, got out a writing pad, tore sheets of paper from it, and with a pencil he wrote something on the first sheet. He wrote slowly, with occasional thoughtful pauses. This is what he had written:

My Father, You know that You have been my only teacher in understanding Your Word, for there has been no other to instruct me. Today, Father, certain words were spoken to me by men who

set limitations on Your powers, and my heart quails
—for who am I to contradict? Therefore, Father, I
here write questions for You to answer, and I
place them before You in humble petition. Reveal
Yourself to me in these matters, Father—for I
must know the truth—or die.

"Following that prayer, Letwaba listed his questions.
They were:

1. Do You heal the sick of body today, as You
did when Jesus was on earth?
2. Is it true, as one man told me today, that
You send sickness to people for their own good?
3. Are Your promises for everyone, or only for
whites?
4. Why do so many of those to whom I've
taken Your message accept it joyously, only to reject it when I am not there to help them to maintain their faith?

"Letwaba then put the sheets of paper on the large
box we used as a table, placed his Bible inside them,
knelt and prayed. Then he drew the stool to the table,
seated himself, opened the Bible and began to read.

"Dusk fell, the hut darkened and I placed a lighted
candle on the table at Letwaba's elbow. He read on
while shadows in the corners of the hut wavered back
and forth as the candle flame flickered. About midnight,
the candle, consumed down to its holder, sputtered a
warning, and I replaced it with another. Still Letwaba
read on, making notes from time to time.

"Shortly after lighting the second candle, I rolled up
in my blanket and slept. I awakened at dawn and saw
Letwaba kneeling, his lifted face alight with quiet happiness, his eyes warm with adoration. I said:

" 'I see that God has spoken to you, Letwaba.'

" 'He has spoken,' Letwaba said, then handed me the notes he'd made during the night, and walked out into the morning.

"Under the question as to whether God heals the sick today, as of yore, he had written:

> *Jesus Christ the same yesterday, and today, and forever.* (Heb. 13:3)
> *For I am the Lord, I change not: . . .* (Mal. 3:6)

"Below the question as to whether God sent sickness were these two quotations:

> *How God (said Peter) anointed Jesus of Nazareth with the Holy Spirit and with power: who went about doing good, and healing all that were oppressed of the Devil; for God was with him.* (Acts 10:38)

"Beside that quotation, Letwaba had penciled a notation: 'Those whom Jesus healed were oppressed of the devil. So those people had not been made sick by God!'

"The second quotation concerned the woman who had a spirit of infirmity for eighteen years, and who was 'bowed together, and who could in no wise lift up herself,' (Luke 13:11) whom Jesus healed, saying:

> *And ought not this woman . . . who Satan hath bound, lo, these eighteen years, be loosed from this bond . . . ?*

"Letwaba's written comment here was: 'Satan had bound her—had made her sick. Jesus healed her.'

"Letwaba's Bible quotations concerning his query as

to whether God's promises were for blacks, as well as whites, were:

> Then Peter opened his mouth and said: Of a truth I perceive that God is no respecter of persons: But in every nation he that feareth Him and worketh righteousness, is accepted with Him. (11 Acts: 34-35)

> Go ye into all the world and preach the Gospel to every living creature. (Mark 16:15)

"Letwaba returned from his walk," Manyao said, "just as I was about to read his notation concerning his request that God show him how to maintain the faith of converts. He took the paper from me, pointed to the Bible quotation beneath the question, and said:

" 'If God ever directed a hand to open a Bible to a needed message, He did so just before daylight. I'd read the New Testament all night with intense concentration, and when I arrived at the second book of Timothy, I was so weary that I feared I could no longer stay awake. So I closed the Bible, placed my hand upon it and prayed that God would direct me to His answer. With my eyes still closed, I opened the Book, and the first verse my eyes fell upon was II Timothy 2:2. With an almost overpowering sense of awe, I read:

> And the things thou hast heard of Me among many witnesses, the same commit thou to faithful men, who shall be able to teach others also.

" 'You see, Manyao,' Letwaba said, 'when I teach in a kraal, I must leave teachers behind me—"faithful men, who shall be able to teach others also." But where shall such men be found? This question I asked of God as I walked in the veldt just now. He answered to my heart: "You must start a Bible school, O Letwaba." '

"And where," Manyao asked, "will you get the money to build such a school?"

" 'When the time has come, God will help me,' Letwaba said. 'But first, I must go on a journey, for I am filled with fire to tell the people that God is the healer of the body as well as of the soul.' "

Letwaba's journey lasted two years. Barefoot and hatless, he wandered far—to the mountain tribes of the Zoutpansberg, to the fever-ridden Mashonas of Rhodesia, to the near-primordial Batshokos and Balambas of the southern Congo, to disease-plagued Basutos and Shangaans and to other tribes. He spoke in hundreds of little villages, where their cattle kraals were enclosed by rocks and spiked thorn branches; he spoke in populous kraals of great chieftains.

His answered prayers for the sick opened the hearts of the people to his message of salvation. In most instances, at news of his coming, whole populations left their cattle and their beer gourds to hear him teach. The story of those years is known to almost everyone south of the Tropic of Capricorn—a marvelous story. More than ten thousand sick were permanently healed, more than one hundred thousand souls brought to Christ.

But there were times when he was met by angry mobs that stoned or beat him—even tried to kill him. This is understandable, for wherever he was permitted to teach, the power of the witch doctors diminished.

"Tremendous" is the word that best describes the results of Letwaba's labors during that two-year pilgrimage; thirty-seven congregations of steadfast Christians were organized in four districts of the Transvaal. The number of congregations in other areas has been estimated by investigators at something over five hundred.

To all of these assemblies, Letwaba promised that as soon as God's time for it had come, he'd open a Bible School in Potgieter's Rust, and there train teachers who would be able to explain the Bible intelligently, and without the fanatical absurdities that often occurred when newly converted primitives misinterpret scriptural passages.

The projected Bible School was a subject of daily prayer during his entire journey. He'd need the Bible School building itself; dormitories for students, a day school for their children, and other buildings essential to such a community. He'd need land, lumber, furnishings; he'd need a constant supply of food for few of his students and their families would have any money at all.

He'd need the support and co-operation of the civic leaders and businessmen of a wide area—men, chiefly of Dutch extraction, who had been reared since childhood in the belief that God had condemned all blacks to eternal servitude.

How to get the land, the money and the co-operation?

Shortly after he arrived in Potgieter's Rust, with the vision of his Bible School warm within him, Letwaba went to a mountaintop and prayed all night. In midmorning, he returned to Potgieter's Rust, went directly to the Town Council told of his hopes for the Bible School and was promptly given sufficient land for his project.

"Any undertaking by such a man as you, Letwaba," one of the Council members said, "will bring this district nothing but good."

Shortly thereafter, Letwaba sent invitations far and wide, to whites and blacks, to attend dedication services for the newly acquired land. He expected only a small group. Instead, people—black and white—came in droves, some walking more than forty miles. In the crowd that listened to his dedication prayer, Letwaba noted many who had been members of mobs who had beaten him years before, and his voice was momentarily choked by tears.

Following his prayer, Letwaba said briefly:

"God will help us to build this school. He will supply the money and other essentials. It may be soon, or it may be long, but in any case, I will not go in debt."

He did not have to.

A farmer in the crowd said: "I've lots of timber growing on my place, Letwaba. Help yourself to all you need."

Two natives stepped forward and said in Suto, "We, O Letwaba, have had experience in saw pits. We will saw your timber into boards, and we will work for God without pay, except sufficient mealie (corn) meal for our porridge."

The pastor of a local church promised furnishings on behalf of his congregation.

A group of white businessmen of Potgieter's Rust, Heidelberg, Sekukuni, declaring that Letwaba's teachings had not only taught them the joy of service to be experienced in business, but that their customers—many of whom had been persuaded to lead the Good Life by Letwaba—were no longer lax in paying their bills, but paid them quickly and eagerly—said through their spokesman:

"This whole section of the Transvaal, Letwaba, is a better and happier place because of you and your teachings. God keep you and guide you, *Friend*."

Within one year, Patmos Bible School was completed, and work on the dormitories—one for men, and one for women—the day school, the kitchens and other outbuildings was well underway.

At about this time, a small farm near Pretoria was given to Letwaba, and his food problem was largely solved, for the farm supplied the basic necessities for native diet—corn, beans and Kaffir corn.

Today more than three thousand graduates of Patmos Bible School are teaching Christianity throughout Africa. Every graduate is deeply spiritual, chosen because he had proved his love for God and for mankind. As a graduate, he specialized for three years in the English and Dutch languages, in church history, in Egyptian, Babylonian, Greek and Roman history, and in the Bible. To gain this graduation certificate, each student must be able to give a clear summary of every chapter of the Bible, and show chapter and verse proof for the ground work of each fundamental doctrine in God's Word.

When a friend of mine asked Letwaba if South Africa's present policy of native oppression wasn't apt to injure his work, Letwaba quoted St. Paul,

Nay, for I am persuaded, that neither death, nor life, nor angels, nor principalities, nor powers, nor things present, nor things to come, nor height, nor depth, nor any other creature shall be able to separate us from the Love of God, which is in Jesus Christ, our Lord. (Romans 9:37-39.)

THE MOST BIZARRE answer-to-prayer story in my collection was told to me by a man named Julian Alco, at a conference of western penologists held in Denver, Colorado. An assignment to cover certain phases of the conference had been given to me by a Scripps-Howard editor, Leon Starmont, who was interested in the road building program for prisoners, originated by Alco. As usually happens when I get into discussions of the problems of daily living, the subject of prayer came up. Alco, a Christian Science practitioner, said:

"One morning an aging Italian came to my office and asked for prayer 'so thata I can maka up my mind.'

" 'Make up your mind about what?' I asked.

" 'I know da name of a man who killa a woman,' he said.

" 'You know a murderer? An uncaught murderer?'

" 'Yes. I know da name. He nica man—no lika to kill. But sometimes he getta too hot in da head. Go a craz'. What to do? This is a nica man when he not craz'. When police catcha heem—zizz—hanga heem by da neck. Dead. No lika dees. You praya, please, so I know to tella da police.'

" 'Look here, John,' I said, 'you don't need prayer to get an anwer to that question. You must go to the police—right now.' I reached for the telephone and said: 'I'll call police headquarters. They'll come here, and you can tell them your story.'

" 'No!' he shouted, and ran from the office.

"Three days later he came back. 'You pray?' he said. 'No? Yes?'

"We knelt together, and I prayed aloud. When John got to his feet, tears were running down his wrinkled *cheeks. His voice was hoarse as he asked: 'Whatta God say?'*

" 'Don't you know, John?'"

" 'Yes. I know. God say thata dees nica man maybe go craz' again an' killa somebody again. Ina my heart I hear God say thata I musta tella da police.'

"Again I reached for the telephone, but John said: 'I go home now. In two days I coma back. Then you calla da police.'

"Two days later he returned, and this time he sat quietly as I dialed police headquarters and asked that an officer be sent to my office. A few minutes later, three detectives from homicide arrived. One of them knew John, and said:

" 'Did you see this killing, John?'

" 'I see.'

" 'And you know the killer?'

" 'I know heem.'

" 'Okay, fellow, who is he?'

" 'Me,' John said."

The Man Who Went to School on the Moon

A FEW DAYS AFTER MARVIN SAXON, PROSPEROUS MEN'S outfitter, arrived at a large eastern penitentiary to begin serving a sentence for manslaughter—he'd caused a fatal accident by falling asleep at the wheel of his car—he was put to work in the prison tailor shop as assistant to Norman Weaver, a coat cutter who was listed in prison records as "incorrigible." Thereupon began a heartwarming answer-to-prayer story.

The story was told to me by Saxon about fifteen years

after he'd finished his sentence and was back managing his clothing business again. As we sat in his balcony office looking out over the main floor of the store, he said:

When I reported to the superintendent of the prison tailor shop that day, he took me over to a cutter's table and introduced me to Weaver. I offered to shake hands, but Weaver, barely glancing at me, went on working, I stood watching a while, then asked:

"What am I supposed to do?"

Weaver didn't even look up.

Angrily, I said: "Can't you answer a civil question?"

Then he looked at me, eyes hard as slate. "Just watch what I'm doing," he said, "because you'll be doing this yourself tomorrow. I'm not going to baby you; I got time of my own to do."

I studied Weaver as I watched him lay paper patterns on cloth, outline them with chalk, then cut along the chalk marks with large black-handled scissors. He seemed to be about my age—thirty—compactly built, with nervous hands and a face as impassive as an Indian's. His mouth was thin lipped and his eyes were sullen. Not until ten minutes before quitting time did he speak to me again, when he said:

"Sweep up around the table. When the four o'clock whistle blows, go out in the Big Yard and line up for chow." Then he walked away, and was at the tailor shop door when the big siren blew for quitting time.

For almost a month Weaver and I worked side by side, seldom exchanging a word. Nevertheless, I'd learned quite a lot about him from other prisoners. Since he'd been in other prisons he was old hand enough to obey most of the rules, but when he thought a guard or a prisoner was imposing on him, he'd fight.

Consequently, he spent a lot of time in the dungeon. He read no books, wrote no letters, attended no classes.

In the meantime, the longer I thought about my conviction, the more I felt it had been unjust. Lots of drivers fall asleep, have accidents, yet don't go to prison. I'd considered myself a good, average Christian, having attended church regularly and contributed generously to collections. I'd said prayers ever since childhood—had even prayed for a light sentence—yet what good had prayers done me? Many a driver had fallen asleep at the wheel, hit someone, and received a light sentence, or no sentence at all. But they'd given me the works. Sheer persecution, I'd told myself—and hatred of the judge who had sentenced me became an obsession. I hated police and the prison officials almost as much.

Convinced I'd been forsaken by men and by Heaven, I developed a bad case of prison blues. When I groused about things to Weaver, he said coldly:

"Look, fellow, don't push your beefs at me. Just do your own time, and let me do mine."

We didn't speak for several days after that, but one Saturday afternoon, a half holiday, as we sat sunning ourselves against a wall in the yard, I burst out:

"I know you hate the world, Weaver, but why do you hate me? I've never done you any harm."

"I don't hate you," he said. "I just don't want any truck with killers."

"Killers? Me? I'm no killer."

"You killed a guy with your car."

"That was an accident, Weaver. And I wasn't drunk, or anything like that—I only fell asleep for a moment—the car swerved, and that old man . . ."

"What's the difference—asleep, or drunk? The guy's dead."

"But . . ."

"Driving liquored up, or full of sleeping pills, or

drugs, or just overtired—it's all the same if it ends in a funeral," he said, and got up and walked away.

I sat there a long time mulling over his words. The chow whistle blew, but I passed up supper. Locked in my cell at last, I sat on the edge of my bunk with one sentence running through my head monotonously: "It's all the same if it ends in a funeral. It's all the same if it ends in a funeral."

Sometime during that night, I wakened with a depressing sense of guilt, but told myself that my victim had really been to blame because, according to a witness, he'd stumbled and fallen when trying to dodge my car. Furthermore, I assured myself, the financial settlement I'd made had been generous enough to pay my debt in full. And if I'd been too weary to drive safely, the old man had certainly been too feeble to be out on the streets, I concluded. Then deciding that we'd been equally to blame, I went back to sleep.

During the following days and nights my sense of guilt kept returning, and my attempts at self-justification became less and less effective. At last came a long, sleepless night when blue devils seemed to dance around my bunk, leering as they mumbled: "It's all the same if it ends in a funeral."

The next afternoon I requested a pass to visit the prison chaplain. I told him my story and ended by saying: "I think I'm going stir-simple, as the prisoners say. Recently, I've been watching some of the murderers in here, and wondering if perhaps I should be doing life as a killer instead of serving a sentence for manslaughter. That doesn't make sense, because no one, looking at my case fully, can say truthfully that it was anything more than a tragic accident. You know, padre, I've got to have help, or . . ." Fear constricted my throat.

"Or what?" the chaplain asked.

"Or blow my top," I nearly shouted.

"Take it easy, man," the padre said. "You won't blow your top. I think what's happening is that you're beginning to see your *real* self now for the first time—and you don't like what you see. Imprisonment does that for some men, and if they've the right stuff in them, they admit their faults and determinedly set their feet on the right road. Let me ask you a question. *Is a man as groggy from lack of sleep, as you were, any more fit to drive a car than a man who's groggy from drink?"*

"That's not a fair question," I said angrily. "A man who falls asleep at the wheel doesn't do it deliberately. Anyway, when he gets in a car it doesn't enter his head that someone might get hurt. A drunk . . ."

"Saxon," the chaplain said, "stop dodging. Drunks don't expect to hurt anyone either."

"But padre . . ." I began.

"Okay, Saxon," he interrupted, "let it rest. I'm not your judge. Nor was the man who sentenced you. You yourself are the real judge, and I pray you'll judge yourself honestly. I've been a chaplain in places like this for a long time. I know how remorse can build up in prisoners. The answer to that is to forget one's self, in helping others. And God knows, there are many men here who need help."

"Yes," I agreed, "many need help."

"That man you work with, for instance."

"Weaver?"

"Yes, Weaver—a poor, lonely, bitter young man."

"How could I help him, padre?"

"I don't know," the chaplain said. "Maybe if you prayed, God would show you how."

"Prayer," I said, getting to my feet, "does no good. I've prayed plenty."

"Only for yourself, most likely—that God would back you up in your opinions of yourself."

"Certainly I've prayed for myself."

"Might try praying for the family of that man your car struck down. Maybe if you prayed for the men in here—for Weaver, for instance—God might be more willing to hear your prayers for yourself. When prayers aren't answered, it's usually one's self that's in the way."

"Could be," I said.

Saturday came again, sunny and warm, and again, Weaver and I sat against the wall in the yard—saying nothing. Actually, Weaver didn't seem to know I was there. For a long time he sat looking up at a flock of pigeons circling above the cell blocks. Once he sighed Then he took an unopened letter from his pocket and began turning it over and over in his hands, brushing the address with his finger tips. There was no hardness or bitterness in his face now—only wistfulness. I said:

"Open it, why don't you?"

"I can't read," he said quietly, after a moment. "I've a bunch of unopened letters in my cell."

"Almost anybody would be glad to read them to you, Weaver."

He nearly shouted. "No!—think I'd let these cons . . .? It's from my mother," he said more quietly. Then he handed me the letter and said: "You're really not a bad Joe, Saxon. You read it to me."

It was a letter filled with love. It spoke of Ruth, Weaver's wife; told about the new rag rug they'd gotten for the apartment. But mostly, it told of Timmie and Ronnie, Weaver's young sons. The last paragraph read:

Timmie and Ronnie keep telling me that you're away having adventures. They want you to hurry home so you can tell them stories like you used to. They talk a lot about one particular story you told—something about a topsy-turvy world on the moon. They're growing fast, Norman. Timmie was four in March, and Ronnie'll be six in June. Now

son, get some friend to write letters for you to your
boys. And please don't worry about us; Ruth and I
both have steady work. We're doing fine, and
we're being patient because we know that someday
our prayers for you will be answered. Our love to
you.

Mother

Weaver took the letter from me, put it in an inside
coat pocket, and said:

"She's a good woman, my mother."

"She loves you," I said.

"I've only known my mother for about four years—
since my last prison term, the one before this one," he
said. "My father was drunken, shiftless. My mother divorced him when I was a baby, and when I was two he
kidnapped me. He was a fruit tramp—followed the harvests—and drank up his earnings. Took me with him
everywhere. When I was six he put me to work picking
cotton. From then on I picked peas here, strawberries
there, apples, beans, apricots, peaches. I never went to
school."

"But your mother . . ."

"My father'd never tell me where she lived. I tried to
remember, but . . ." He stopped abruptly.

"Go on," I said. "Tell me about Timmie and Ronnie—and Ruth."

"Lay off me," he said shortly, jumped to his feet and
disappeared in a crowd of milling prisoners.

Not once during the next work morning did Weaver
speak to me, but when the noon whistle blew, he said:

"I'm not eating. I'm staying here in the shop."

"I'm not hungry either," I said. "I'll stay with you."

He fussed and fidgeted, picked up scissors and put

them down again. At last he took a folded sheet of writing paper from his pocket.

"This was in one of the letters I opened last night in my cell," he said. He held it out to me. Ronnie'd written it in a first-grader's awkward letters. I read it aloud:

Timmie found a cat. It is black. It drinks milk, and it is fat. It is a sleepy cat. Its name is Kitty. When are you coming home? I am lonesome.

At the bottom of the page, Timmie'd printed in higgledy-piggledy letters:

I am four. I will drive a truck. I am hugging you. I had a birthday party.

Weaver had turned his back and was fiddling with a piece of cloth on the cutting table. I laid the letter on the cloth.

"Okay now, beat it," Weaver said.

"Those kids, Weaver," I said. "What kind of guy are you—not getting someone to write to those lonely kids for you?"

He whirled on me, white faced. "How can I write to them? he asked bitterly. "They write better than I can. Do you think I want them to know I am an ignorant lout? I want those kids to think about me like other kids think about their fathers. I want . . ." He threw his arms wide in a helpless gesture. "I'm mixed up," he said. "Nobody can understand."

"We've an educational department here, Weaver," I said. "You could attend beginner's class. It wouldn't be long before . . ."

"No!" he shouted. "No! You don't understand!"

"Well, I understand this much," I said. "I understand that you're acting like a simpleton, Weaver. You could learn to write in no time—they'll even let you off work to attend those classes. Or I could teach you myself, in the yard after work."

Weaver looked suddenly sick. He took a deep breath, then said:

"The minute I even think about going to school, I get all fuzzy—frightened. I—well—I went to school once or twice, but I couldn't even get to 'G.'"

"What's 'G'?"

"A-B-C- up to G."

"The alphabet. Why not, Weaver? I don't get it."

"I just can't get past 'G,' that's all. I can't get past 'G,'" he said, and walked away.

That afternoon, Weaver was thrown in the dungeon for swearing at a guard. When he came back to work after nine days on bread and water, his mood was so black that at the first opportunity, I went to the prison psychiatrist about him.

"During the routine psychological examination given Weaver when he was admitted here," he said, "he answered most of our questions with lies. He's so antagonistic toward authority that we've classified him as a potential habitual criminal."

"I'd like to help him," I said.

"So would all of us. But Weaver doesn't want to be helped. We did persuade him to start school when he first came in. He can't read even the simplest words, you know. At his very first class, the instructor bent over him to show him how to print the letters of the alphabet. Weaver suddenly jumped to his feet, struck the instructor in the face and rushed from the room. He lost six months' 'good time' for that beef. There are lots of men in here, Saxon, who'd appreciate your interest in them. Why waste time on Weaver?"

Another week passed with no change in Weaver. I'd seen enough of his better side to know it was really there, and I felt that although it was shut away deep inside him, no complicated psychiatric folderol was needed to bring it into the open. Weaver was a simple soul, I told myself, and perhaps the gadget that would free him was as simple as he."

Two or three times during the next few weeks, I considered the idea of giving up on Weaver, but each time the thought of his kids intruded. I just couldn't quit. However, I was getting nowhere fast, so halfheartedly I went to talk things over with the chaplain again. He was on vacation, but substituting for him was a very old man with kindly eyes—Abel Williamson, a retired minister. He knew nothing about Weaver, and didn't bother to look him up in the files, but after listening to me with interest, he took a red-letter testament from the drawer of his desk, handed it to me and said:

"Persuade Weaver to read this, particularly Jesus' own words—the words printed in red. He'll find, if he reads prayerfully . . ."

"But Weaver can't read," I said.

"Well then, my boy, you read it to him. It'll do you both good."

"Mr. Williamson," I said, "I doubt that Weaver will let me read it to him. Even if he would, he'd probably not understand it."

"He'll understand," Williamson answered. "That's the beauty of Jesus' own teachings—anybody can understand them. I was a missionary in China for many years, and I still have to meet the man—ignorant or erudite—who can't understand: *Love thy neighbor as thyself, and love thy God with thine whole heart.* Jesus taught largely in parables, you know, because most of the people to whom he was speaking were as ignorant as Weaver is. Certainly if the poor and uneducated of Jesus' day could understand Him, the poor and uneducated of today can also. Perhaps if you brought Weaver to see me . . ."

That night in my cell as I sat on the bunk listening to the cacophony of musical instruments and phonographs being played by inmates along the cell rows, I took the red-letter testament from the small stand where I'd put it and began glancing through it, reading bits here and there, flipping pages haphazardly. My attention centered on a passage that began:

Inasmuch as ye have done it unto one of the least of these my brethren, ye have done it unto me.

I glanced back a few verses and read:

For I was hungered and ye gave me meat; I was thirsty and ye gave me drink; I was a stranger and ye took me in; Naked and ye clothed me: I was sick and ye visited me: I was in prison, and ye came unto me.

The twanging of guitars, the blaring of brass instruments, the hotcha music faded from my consciousness as I turned back to the third chapter of Matthew, to Jesus' first spoken words and started to read. I was completely absorbed in the heart-lifting story of understanding and love, and was still reading—lost to everything but the New Testament story—when taps sounded and the cell light went off for the night.

The next morning as Weaver and I sat on the cutting table waiting for a new batch of cloth to be brought to us, I took the red-letter testament from my pocket and began thumbing through it. Weaver eyed the little book, then said:

"I've got a book exactly like that one in my cell. My

mother sent it to me with a letter. I've still got the letter, too."

"You know, Weaver," I said, "I had the idea that if you'd let me read this testament to you it might help you see how foolish you are not to learn to read and write while you've got a chance. And I figured it might help you in other ways. It hadn't struck me that I'd be helped by reading it, but I was—it's the most helpful book ever written."

"About God, isn't it?"

"It's about Jesus when He was on earth. He's God's son, you know."

"Heard all about it in a mission when I was hiding out on Skid Row in Seattle one time. Used to sit in that mission for hours, keeping out of the rain. The preacher used to say Jesus was always helping out bums and doxies. I got real interested, but one night the cops raided the joint where I was hiding, and I did thirty days for vag. Yeah, I remember I was real interested. But that was a long time ago, just after I got out of reform school. The cops framed Jesus, didn't they?"

"I guess you could call it that. Palestine, where Jesus lived, was governed by the Romans. At His trial, Jesus was found 'not guilty' of breaking Roman laws, but instead of turning Him loose, the judge—his name was Pilate—turned Him over to the high priests, who were the bosses of the Hebrew church. They condemned Him to be crucified—nailed to a cross—because He'd said He was the Son of God."

"What did He want to say that for?"

"Because He *was* the Son of God. Oh, the priests gave Him a chance to go free—all He'd have had to do was say that He *wasn't* God's Son. But he wouldn't say that, so He died."

"Maybe I don't want you to read that book to me.

It's a sad story. I already feel sad most of the time. Ain't
you got a happy story?"

I saw that Jesus' story had captured Weaver's sympathy, and I prayed silently that God would help me tell
the rest of it in a way Weaver could understand. After a
moment's thought, I said:

"Yes, it's a sad story in a way, but it's also the hap-
piest story you'll ever hear. You see, Weaver, Jesus really was the Son of God. He'd been sent to earth to
show people the way to peace and happiness. He saw
people trying every which way to find true happiness—saw that the poor were bitter with envy of the
rich, that the rich were bitter with the knowledge that
despite all their money they were just as unhappy as the
poor. He saw, too, that the powerful—the rulers, the
bosses, the priests—were as unhappy as all the rest.
Jesus knew the secret of happiness, and He spent all His
time telling that secret to anyone who'd listen. Some listened and believed, but many—particularly the rich and
the powerful—wouldn't have any part of the secret, and
ordered Him to lay off—or else."

"And He wouldn't, so they killed Him. Oh, well, it
was a nice try," Weaver said.

Rain fell the rest of that week, but Saturday was
warm and sunny. After noontime chow, Weaver and I
found a secluded spot beside the cell-block wall and settled down on the yard pavement for the afternoon. I
took the testament from my pocket, and wondering if
Weaver'd still be in the mood to be read to, said:

"Okay fellow, open your ears."

Weaver fumbled in his inside coat pocket, brought
out his own testament and said, handing it to me: "I'd
kinda like you to read out of this one."

I opened it to the flyleaf, and read aloud his mother's
inscription:

Behind the cloud the starlight lurks,
Through showers the sunbeams fall;
For God, who loveth all His works,
Has left His hope with all.

I said: "Mothers never lose hope, I guess."

"Doggone," Weaver said.

And so it was, sitting in the yard during work-free hours, that I read the New Testament to Weaver. He didn't just listen to the story—he *lived* it. He mumbled angrily when King Herod decreed the death of the babies; chortled gleefully when Mary, Joseph and Jesus escaped the massacre. At times Weaver listened silently; sometimes he laughed. Sometimes his eyes held tears. When Pilate handed Jesus over to be crucified, Weaver got angry. During the Crucifixion scene, he sat tensely grim. As the story of the Resurrection ended, he said:

"He sure outsmarted the mobsters that time."

When Weaver asked questions I wasn't able to answer, we'd go over to the chaplain's office and put them to Mr. Williamson, who obviously liked Weaver, and answered without talking down to him. One day in a burst of appreciation to the old gentleman, Weaver said:

"You're a good John, parson, and if there's anybody in this joint does you wrong, just let me know and I'll shiv him for you."

"You're a good Joe yourself, Weaver," Williamson said. "And once upon a time, perhaps I'd have appreciated your offer. But not any more, not since I decided to love instead of hate. You remember that Jesus said to love your neighbor, don't you?"

"Sure."

"And to love your enemies?"

"Yeah, I remember that, too."

"And those who persecute you?"

"Yeah, He said that, but He didn't mean we should love cops and screws and prison rats, did He? Did He?"

"Yes, He did. He meant exactly that. Oh, I know a man can't just say he's going to love somebody who's treated him harshly, or meanly, or unfairly, but a man can ask God to put love in his heart, and God will do it. Stop hating, my boy. Hate destroys the hater in the end. Be smart, young fellow. Living the way Jesus tells us to live is the way to all of the things that really matter in life."

"So I'm to try and love the bulls that go out of their way to make me do tough time—the screws that beat me when they throw me in the dungeon. That it?"

"With God's help, yes."

"Doggone!" Weaver said.

About a month after that talk with Williamson, Captain Fowler, the guard in charge of the tailor shop, called me into his office, shut the door, motioned me to a chair, seated himself at his desk, and said:

"I've been a prison guard for a long time, Saxon, and if I've learned anything about the Big House, it's that the best way to stop trouble is to stop it before it starts. I'm not asking you to rat, Saxon, but I am asking for information that might help me head off what could be a beef blowing up. What's this guy Weaver up to?"

"Weaver? Up to?"

"Look, Saxon. When a con-wise, prison-broke guy like Weaver—who's worked out a routine that enables him to do his time the easiest way—switches to a new routine overnight, there are only three reasons. He's making a play for better consideration by the parole board; planning some shenanigans; or going stir-simple. Weaver won't be due for the parole board for a long time. He's certainly not going stir-simple. So, the only answer left is that he's up to something—and something from Weaver means something bad. So, what's he planning?"

"You're talking Greek," I said. "Weaver's not planning anything out of line."

"Maybe not, but maybe yes. Month after month, Weaver's made his daily task—never more, never less. Now for three weeks or so, he's doing a daily stint of from one to four units more than the task set. That guy wouldn't give the prison a single breath more than he had to. So all of a sudden, he becomes overproductive. What's he up to, Saxon?"

"Get set for a shock, Mr. Fowler," I said. "Weaver's trying an experiment. He's trying to be a good con. Weaver's been reading the Bible."

"Another crack like that, Saxon, and you're in the hole," Fowler said. "Weaver can't even read his own name."

"I've been reading the New Testament to him in off hours, Mr. Fowler, and Mr. Williamson—who's sitting in for the chaplain—has been explaining Jesus' message to Weaver. Weaver figures now that hatred hasn't got him anything, so he's trying to play it the other way. He's not doing more than the daily stint to make a showing; it's only because he's beginning to feel sort of hopeful inside."

"You cons," Fowler said. "The things you think up! Okay, beat it—I've had my laugh for today."

Back at the cutting table, I answered Weaver's questioning look by explaining that Fowler'd been checking work sheets, and had noticed we'd been making more than task. "He thought maybe we were working an angle." I said.

Weaver laughed. "Guards get stir-simple when they've been on the job a long time," he said. "But Fowler's not a bad lug—as guards go."

That was the first time I'd ever heard Weaver say a good word for a guard.

A few days later, Weaver brought me two letters to read to him. One was from his mother, the other from Ruth. Both letters were newsy with little things—new blankets for the boys' beds, a new clothesline, the old washing machine repaired at last, plans for a birthday party for Ronnie, a retread for the Ford, and cheerful plans for the family when Weaver was discharged. An enclosure, written by Ruth, but signed by Timmie and Ronnie, said:

> We got a prize in a breakfast food package. It is a sheriff's badge. We are saving it for you for a Christmas present when you get home. It is a surprise.

When I'd finished reading, Weaver was white lipped. I said:

"You've just got to stop horsing around about your family, Weaver—you've got to let me write to them for you. You can give me permission to write, or not; either way, I'm going to get word to them that you're in good health. You know, fellow, I don't get you—you love your family—every one of them. Yet, you act as if you never wanted to see them again."

"I don't," Weaver said.

"Don't what?"

"I don't want to see them again. I've brought them nothing but grief. I'm a three-time loser. One more rap, and I'll be a habitual, and doing it all—life."

"This is your last rap, Weaver," I said. "You know it, and I know it. You've learned that there's a better way to live than to be always fighting the law. Your attitude's crazy, and you know it."

"Yeah, crazy," Weaver said. "But there's more to it

—something inside of me. My family's tops . . . but I'm a crumb. Don't you think my kids'll spot me for what I am one of these day? I . . ."

"Well, what are you?"

"I'm no account—I'm poor white trash. I'm dumb, ignorant—can't even write my name. Already, my kids know more about schooling than I'll ever learn."

"The answer to that seems an easy one, Weaver," I said. "Just stop being ignorant and dumb. A year in the primary grades in the educational department here is about all you'll need to cure your feelings of inferiority. In prison schools you can learn just as fast as you want to, you know."

"I can't go to school," he said, "I go all to pieces—I can't get past 'G.' When I get to 'G' I get sick—sick. Sick in the head, mostly."

"Here we go again," I said.

"Lay off me, convict," Weaver said hoarsely. I saw he was trembling, and let the matter drop, but at the first opportunity, I took the 'G' business up with Chaplain Williamson.

"Bring Weaver here on Sunday morning after church," he said. "There's something eating at the boy, some psychological quirk. Let's see if we can't open him up."

However, Weaver couldn't keep the Sunday appointment—he was in the dungeon again for insulting a guard. Again he did nine days on bread and water. "But, Saxon," he said, "I found out for sure that this business of loving the bulls won't work."

He made the same statement to Mr. Williamson when he met with him in his office two Sundays later. Williamson said:

"God didn't mean that we must love the *things* that some men do. He meant we must look beyond those things, into a man's secret heart—to the divine spark that is always there no matter how dimly buried under fear, hate, greed, ignorance and selfishness. It's this spark of God that we must love, for by loving that in a man, we cause it to glow—sometimes to burst into flame that devours the trash beneath which it has lain. That guard you insulted has that divine spark exactly as everyone else has. Why did you insult him?"

"I didn't. When I stepped out of the mess-hall line for a moment that day, he said he'd have me thrown in the dungeon. All I said to him was:

"'Watch your blood pressure, sweetheart.' So he ran me to the Captain's office, told the usual lies, and the Captain slipped me nine days. It isn't the dungeon I mind, Parson, it's the way some of those con-minded guards go out of their way to make it tough for me. Down in that dark hole I had plenty of time to think of the things cops have done to me—frame-ups, beatings . . ."

"Yes, yes," Williamson said, and motioned us to chairs. When we'd settled down, he turned to Weaver:

"I've talked to a lot of prisoners in here, Weaver, and I find that most of them class all cops as bad, because a few were. It's like the folks who hate all Jews because they had trouble with one—like people who hate all Arabs because one Arab gave them a bad time —hate all Frenchmen because of one. How many guards really bear down too hard on inmates?"

"Look, Parson," Weaver said angrily, "I've been through it—you ain't. In reform school, they beat my bare backside with a four-inch-wide leather strap, and in the strap were half-inch holes. That strap raised blisters of purple flesh. The pain was so great that I fainted at the third blow. Know why they beat me like that? 'Cause I couldn't learn my A B C's."

"Couldn't, or wouldn't?"

"Couldn't, Parson. There's something wrong with my

head when it comes to schooling. Anyway, I ran away. Two days later, a farmer found me hiding in a haystack and took me back. So they beat me again—with a flat board that broke every blister. When I got well enough to walk, they put me back in school, but I couldn't learn any better than at first, so they finally gave it up and put me to work peeling spuds. And I peeled spuds for almost two years—until my discharge.

"I went on the bum for a while, and got by until I hit a big town where I met a man who offered me a job as helper on a truck—told me to meet him that night at a certain place. I did, and we rolled out of town. At the outskirts of the next town, police picked us up because the truck was loaded with stolen cigarettes. My boss copped a plea, but I kept telling the bulls I didn't have any idea the truck was stolen. They kept after me to cop a plea, too, but I wouldn't, so they took me into a room and beat a guilty plea out of me. When they found I was only sixteen, they sent me to another reform school. But that time I was prison wise and stayed clear of beatings. That place didn't send me to school, but put me to work weaving chair bottoms. I had lots of time to work up a good hate for bulls. Wanna hear more, Parson?"

"I've seen your record, Weaver, but yes, go ahead."

"When I was turned loose, I began hitting the harvests—worked in the grapes and hops in California; apples in Oregon; vegetables in the Imperial Valley; even worked in the peas, in Michigan. It was in the wheat in Montana, though, that I got caught burglarizing a grocery store, and made the Big House. I did the full five years without parole. Know why?" He bent his head toward Williamson, and said: "Feel that dent under the hair? That's where a prison guard slugged me with a heavy cane because I was fighting with another con. Fractured my skull, and lost me my 'good time' credits.

"When I was turned loose I beat my way to another state, got a job in a gas station, and stayed clean. You know—stayed away from losers, became an Honest John. It paid off, too, because I met Ruth and we got married. She knew my record and figured I'd stay straight, you see. We got a little house, and Ronnie and Timmie came along. In the meantime, I'd located my mother, and she came to live with us. And we were all as happy as singing birds.

"One afternoon a panel truck rolled in for a grease job. I told the driver it'd take a half an hour, so he walked off down the street for a cup of coffee and didn't come back. That night I ran the truck into an old shed on an adjoining lot—figuring the driver'd come back the next morning. He still hadn't shown up at 10:00 A.M., but two motorcycle policemen did. They pulled in for gas, spotted the panel truck in the shed and checked its license plate with a list they had in a notebook. Suddenly one of them threw a gun on me, and the other walked over and jerked open the truck's doors. It was filled with cases of cigarettes.

"Well, I was arrested and charged with being an accomplice in the theft of the truck and its load. I told my story exactly as it happened, but the cops laughed at it. The driver never was caught. I'd already done time for one cigarette beef, so what chance did I have? I got five years—and here I am."

"Yes, here you are," Williamson said. "You've been in trouble with the law since you were thirteen, according to your record. What I'd like to know is how you got sent to reform school in the first place."

"Don't do any good to talk about it, Parson. Anyway, I've talked too much already. Let's skip the whole thing."

"I've a reason for wanting to know your whole story,

Weaver. Anyway, you've been in a shell for too long—you'll feel better for talking. Tell me."

"You're a funny guy, Parson," Weaver said, "and I'll level with you, even if I don't understand why you're interested in me—just another no-account con."

"You know why I'm interested, all right. It's because there's enough good in you to make you the man you were meant to be, Weaver. Now let's have the rest of your story."

Weaver was silent—staring at the floor. When he looked up again, his eyes were moist. Williamson and I pretended not to notice, and after a few moments, Weaver said:

"My father was a drunk, and ran off with me when my mother divorced him. He became a harvest tramp, and little as I was, I worked alongside of him until I was twelve. Sometimes the only clothing I had was an old shirt of my old man's—no pants, no shoes—nothing but the shirt. Every once in a while authorities would say I had to go to school. When that happened, we'd flit. When I was eleven, the old man got a steady job with a cotton sharecropper, and we lived in a shack without doors or windows. My friends were Negro kids, and every one of them was better off than I was—their fathers didn't drink much; mine drank up every cent we earned. When I was twelve, my old man got sent up for stealing a sheep, and I never saw him again. I hung around the shack for a couple of weeks, then a Negro woman, called Auntie Lindy, took me to her house, gave me a pretty good pair of pants and told me I had to go to school with her kids—she had six kids.

"The school was a one-room school with about thirty kids. All eight grades took turns going to a bench at the front of the room to recite. I was put in the first grade with three little Negroes—all about six or seven. Like I said, I was twelve, lean and gawky, and I felt like a fool up there with those smart little shavers. They seemed smart to me, at least, because they could already read about the hen that sat on her nest, and the mouse that lived in the city. Me, I couldn't read a lick.

"The teacher was a white man named Lane, who coughed all the time, and he was meaner than—well, meaner than a Gila monster. He kept a heavy stick beside his desk, and when one of the kids goofed his lesson, that teacher'd baste him a couple of good ones.

"Because I was a white boy, poorer and dumber than even the smallest black kids, I felt ashamed all the time. I'd get so ashamed that my head would feel hot inside. The teacher put me to learning my A B C's, and I thought I was doing fine because I could say them up to 'F.' But I guess the teacher didn't think I was doing so hot because one morning when I was looking out the window, dreaming about swimming down in the creek, he called me a dirty wood's colt and poor white trash. Seems he'd spoken to me and I hadn't heard him. Anyway, all the kids laughed, and I was so ashamed that I started to cry. That made me more ashamed, and I felt my head getting hot inside again. He called me to the front of the room, and said:

" 'Start reciting, Wood's Colt.'

" 'A-B-C-D-E-F!' I said, and there I stuck.

" 'Go on,' the teacher said, and reached for his stick.

" 'A-B-C-D-E-F!' I said, and stuck again.

"The teacher grabbed me by the shirt collar and whammed me over the head. All of a sudden everything went fuzzy—sort of red—and screaming like a wild crow, I lit into him—scratched his face and kicked him in the stomach. Then I ran—ran through a cotton field, across some plowed ground, through a wood lot—and kept on running.

"Sometime that afternoon I holed up in some brush until it got dark, then took off, heading north. I was hungry as a new-shed snake, and about midnight filled up on onions from a field. Just before daylight I holed up in a haystack and stayed there all day, sick in my stomach. That's the way it went for about six days— traveling at night, eating from fields and orchards. One early morning an old gray-haired Negro caught me coming out of an outhouse where I'd slept, and I was too sick and weak to run any longer. He was a nice old fellow though, and he hitched up his mule, drove me to the edge of a big city, gave me eleven cents and said good-by. I walked up an alley, saw a baker's cart and spent ten cents for ginger bread—it had white frosting on it. I was afraid to go into the city, so I hung around that alley all the rest of the day. Some woman got suspicious of me and called the cops, and I don't know exactly what happened after that. I remember they fed me good, and took me before a man with a red face and a big nose. He was nice, but I was scared they'd send me back to that teacher if I told the truth, so I made up a lot of lies. I slept in jail that night, and the next day a woman took me about fifty miles—to the reform school. Like I already told you, Parson, they tried to make me learn my A B C's, and all of a sudden I got that same feeling that made me fight the teacher, and—well, you know the rest."

"I'm glad you've told me this, Weaver," Williamson said. "But now it's almost time to line up for mess. Will you come back and see me again soon, my boy?"

"I don't want no chow," Weaver said.

Williamson looked at me. "Neither do I," I said.

For several minutes Williamson sat with closed eyes, and I wondered if he were praying. At last he said:

"I've listened to you, Weaver, and now I hope you'll listen to me."

"I'll listen," Weaver said.

"It's about your hatred of bulls, as you call them,"

Williamson began. "As I've told you, you've the makings in you of the man you really want to be—good husband—good father—good son. That's what you'd be if you knew how, isn't it?"

"Yes, more than anything. But it's not in the cards, Parson. I've tried—tried to stop hating the bulls, and all, but the more I try to like them, the more I hate their guts."

"You hate them, Weaver, because you fear them."

"Afraid? Me? Nuts!"

"Man can't hate what he doesn't fear. Maybe you don't fear them physically—I don't think you do. But you *do* fear them for what they're able to do to make you mean, and contrary, and antagonistic. Oh, I don't expect you to understand all that psychological complications of your hatreds, Weaver, and it isn't necessary that you do. The whole thing can be explained clearly and simply—if God will give me the right words.

"Weaver, Jesus didn't mean that one must love the *things* people do—as I said before. He meant that deep down inside each one of us is the man made in His own image—the man we must love—the man who'd also love, if he knew how."

"It's no use, Parson—I keep thinking of the ways cops have done me wrong, and . . ."

"Did the authorities do Jesus wrong?"

"Yeah. And if I'd been there with a Tommy gun . . ."

"There were lots of men in Jerusalem who felt the same way, Weaver—men who'd gladly have rushed the soldiers and taken Jesus from them. But that wasn't the Way of the Cross."

"You mean Jesus *wanted* to be crucified?"

"Jesus came to earth to live as a human, Weaver. He endured the same pain, trials, tribulations and sorrows that all men endure. He was reviled, cursed and persecuted. He knew poverty, cold and insecurity. But He also knew love of mother, father, brothers and friends. He'd been a carpenter, and He'd walked hundreds of miles giving His message, so He was strong and healthy and virile. When the money-lenders profaned the temple, Jesus didn't need help to drive them out—He went after them singlehanded. The human side of Him loved life—didn't want to die on the Cross, and the human side of Him prayed in the Garden of Gethsemane that God would let Him evade the physical agonies in store for Him. But God reminded Him that if His message to the world was to live forever, He must go through with His sacrifice. Suffering unto death was the one way He could prove to mankind that He truly loved us.

"So He let the soldiers arrest Him. He heard the people jeer Him as He half carried, half dragged, the heavy cross to Golgotha—the Hill of the Skulls. He walked with blood trickling over His face from a crown of thorns that had been scoffingly jammed on His head. At the place of crucifixion, when the cross was placed flat on the ground, Jesus—without protest—lay down upon it and stretched out His arms. Nor did He protest when they drove nails through His hands and feet, and planted the cross upright.

"It took long for Him to die, and His sufferings became so unbearable that once He cried:

" 'My God, my God, why hast thou forsaken me?'

"That was the human side of Him, crying to be relieved of His physical agonies.

"The hours wore on, and still death lingered. But not once did Jesus show anger nor hate against His murderers. Instead, near the end of His suffering, He called upon God to forgive His enemies because they didn't know what they were doing.

"Now, Weaver, we're not forced to accept Jesus' message of love—we are free to reject it. But those who reject it are crucifying Jesus all over again. In that red-letter testament of yours, in the last three verses of the eleventh chapter of Matthew, you'll find Jesus' gentle, kindly urging of you—of me—of everyone—to accept the peace of soul that He won for us on Calvary. Here, my boy, is what He says:

> Come unto me, all ye that labor and are heavy laden, and I will give you rest. Take my yoke upon you, and learn of me; for I am meek and lowly in heart; and ye shall find rest unto your souls. For my yoke is easy, and my burden is light. (Matt. 11:28, 29, 30.)

"Look, Parson," Weaver said, "you make it sound easy. But I seem to remember that mission preacher on Seattle's Skid Row telling us that all of Jesus' top men were gunned down by mobsters, or strung up at lynch parties. I ain't arguing, you understand, and I gotta hunch that if I wasn't such a louse, Jesus could make me a right guy. But, if His way's so easy, how come a lot of the men that He sent out to preach ended up the hard way?"

"I assume you're speaking of the apostles. Yes, it's true that most of them were killed because they carried Jesus' message of love. But, Weaver, those who died were glad to give their lives for the good of humanity. Is a life so much to pay for bringing God to *millions?*"

"Were all the apostles killed?"

"All but one of the first group of apostles were. Let's see—Matthew was killed with a sword. Mark was dragged through the streets until he died. Luke was hanged on an olive tree in Greece. John was put into a kettle of boiling oil, in Rome, but it didn't kill him; he died a natural death, much later, in Asia. James the Greater, was beheaded in Jerusalem. James the Less, was thrown from a temple tower, then beaten to death with a club. Philip was hanged in Phrygia. Bartholomew was skinned alive. Andrew was tied to a cross, and he preached to the spectators until he died. Thomas was run through the body with a lance. Jude was shot to death by arrows. Simon the Zealot was crucified in Persia. Matthias was stoned, then beheaded. Barnabas was stoned to death. Paul was beheaded in Rome. Peter is thought to have been crucified, but that's not certain.

"Millions throughout the centuries, Weaver, have been killed in one way or another, in attempts to stop the preaching of God's message of love. Someday, Weaver, that message will conquer the world."

"Parson," Weaver said, "I think I'm beginning to understand. All of a sudden, my hates seem sorta chippy." He sighed deeply. "I wish I could read the Bible for myself," he said. "Then maybe my kids wouldn't feel about me like I feel about my old man—ashamed."

The lockup whistle blew—it blew early on Sundays —and Weaver and I hurried to the cell block. As the steel door shut me in for the night, I was thinking that Williamson's talk had been as much for me, as for Weaver. Humbly, I knelt by my bunk.

Next morning I got up before the rising bell rang, wrote Weaver's mother a comforting letter and dropped it in the yard mailbox. Instead of going to the mess hall at noon, I went to the educational department and signed Weaver up for first grade schoolwork. During a work-break that afternoon, I said to Weaver:

"Starting tomorrow, you're going to begin school— an hour each afternoon—and you're going to learn to read and write. I'm sick of hearing you can't get past 'G.' "

I expected Weaver to blow up at me. Instead, he agreed, and the next afternoon, he began his lessons. During the third session, he practically blew his top— shouted at the convict teacher, brushed his primer, paper and pencil to the floor—and staggered from the building. In front of the hospital, Dr. Earl Watkins, one of the staff, nodded to him, did a double-take, and said:

"Are you in pain, fellow?"

Weaver snarled at him, started to move on, but paused, trembling, then sat weakly on the hospital steps. Dr. Watkins pulled him to his feet and helped him into a consultation room. Just a minute or two before the quitting whistle blew, Weaver came back to the job. I said:

"You must have had a long lesson."

"No, I blew my top again," he said. "I'm through with school for good."

"I figured you for having guts, Weaver," I said angrily, "and it turns out you're as flabby as boiled macaroni."

"I've been with Dr. Watkins," he said. "He asked me questions for more than an hour. I told him just about all I know about myself. When I got up to leave, he said: 'You're a lot sicker than you know, Weaver, and school makes it worse, so lay off the studies.'"

"Okay, Weaver," I said, "I'm through," and walked away from him.

That night in my cell I did a lot of thinking about Weaver, and the more I thought, the more disgusted I was with his seeming spinelessness. At the same time, I was angry with Dr. Watkins, who, I felt, had cut the ground out from under me.

Next day, when Weaver and I—not talking at all—were comfortably ahead on the day's task, I went to Captain Fowler and got permission to visit Dr. Watkins.

"This guy Weaver, Doctor," I said. "I've been working on him for months to get him to go to school. Then you come along and undo all my work. Did you really tell him to stop studying?"

"I did."

"All right," I said, "so the guy's got some sort of mental block because his first schoolteacher whammed him over the head while he was reciting the alphabet. It's my opinion that he's only babying himself—and you're helping him do it."

"You're wrong, Saxon, very wrong. It isn't as simple as that. To force Weaver to go to school is as cruel as it would be to force a shell-shocked soldier to return, uncured, to the front lines. Weaver's mental block, as you call it, goes back much farther than that episode with the teacher—far, far back. You—like all would-be amateur psychologists—jump at the obvious, give it importance it does not have, work out some sort of procedure for cure, and, of course, are wrong. You're a destructive and pestilent breed, Saxon."

"Well, Doctor," I said, "if it wasn't that beating by his teacher—what was it?"

"I don't know. Weaver doesn't know. He may never find out. Certainly he's not likely to find out in this place, where there's no time for deep analysis. Weaver's a sick man—in school."

"I guess I don't understand," I said.

"Nor do I, fully, Saxon. However, in his childhood, Weaver was subjected to painful assaults and numerous other pernicious episodes. His body dealt with those threats to his happiness in certain ways, such as reduction in capillary tone, flooding of tissues with liquid, cessation of digestion, and other defense measures. In time, those reactions became a pattern, and when he's under stress, his body resorts to that pattern again."

"And determination—will power—won't help?"

"No more than it will help shell shock."

"Then what will help? I mean, what can I do to? . . ."

"Just stop pestering him, Saxon," the doctor said. "You only make him worse."

When I left Dr. Watkins I was pretty sick myself—

my hopes for Weaver's education had not only gone by the board, but I felt also that prayer had failed. Disheartened, I dropped in to Mr. Williamson's office and told him about my interview with Watkins. He listened without interrupting until I was through, then said:

"You've been making this whole Weaver situation too complicated, Saxon. God's miracles are never complicated, nor do they always involve extraordinary methods. Miracles are made of simple things—and faith. Now, my boy, bow your head and listen as I pray:

" 'God,' he said, 'we place Weaver's case in Your hands. We will not judge him, nor will we try to force our ideas on him. Open the way, Father, that Weaver may study without the reactions that have plagued him. We leave the problem with You, in faith that You will solve it. And help us, Lord, to work in harmony with You. Amen.' "

I was on the porch, on my way out, when Williamson came to the door and said:

"God will answer, Saxon. Keep praying."

"Yes, sir," I said.

Weaver's cure began the next day.

At noon, after we'd left the mess hall, I stopped at the library to pick up a book, and Weaver waited for me in the lobby. When I came out he was studying a poster depicting a man gazing at the moon through a telescope.

"Some guy's going to lecture here Saturday on the solar system," I said. "That big ball's a picture of the full moon."

"I know that," he smiled. "I used to live there."

"What?" I said.

"When I was a kid I used to pretend I lived on the moon. To get there, all I had to do was go outside our shack, look up, flap my arms once, then shoot up into the sky like a rocket. The moon was always warm and bright when I got there, and everybody was happy and good. All that the kids did was play all day long because there was no field work to do there. I even knew the King of the Moon. He was kind of a gold color, and he liked me." He sighed. "That was a long time ago," he said wistfully.

"Tell me some more about the moon, Weaver."

"Aw, that was kid stuff," he said as we headed toward the tailor shop.

"I had daydreams like that when I was a boy, Weaver," I said. "I used to pretend I could swim in the air. I'd sit in school and imagine I was swimming slowly around above the other kids' heads, and that they were looking at me with wonder. Sometimes I'd swim right out through a window and float around up above the schoolhouse. It was fun."

Weaver's face brightened. "That's the way I got around on the moon sometimes," he said, "swimming in the air."

"I guess most kids have swimming and flying daydreams," I said, "but I didn't know any who imagined they lived on the moon. What else did you do up there?"

Weaver didn't answer until we'd laid out some patterns and had begun cutting cloth. Then he said:

"When I was about seven, my old man took me to Alabama where he'd got a job in the goobers—peanuts. We lived in an abandoned shack on the edge of a gum wood. The shack had no door because the old man split it up for firewood. At that place they wouldn't let little kids in the goober fields, so I stayed around the shack all day by myself. I didn't go into the wood, because the colored kids had told me it was haunted. I wasn't too lonely in the daylight, but when night came I wanted my father—even if he was mean drunk. Lots of nights, though, he didn't come home at all, and I slept on the floor, keeping warm by burning dry cow chips in sort of a stove the old man had made from a five-gallon oilcan he'd picked off some garbage dump.

"One night as I lay there afraid to sleep, a big, fat, old yellow moon came floating into the sky. I was pretty miserable, and wished I could go and live on the moon and never come back. I lay on the ground a long time, watching the moon sail higher and higher, and wishing harder and harder that I knew a way to get up there. Then all of a sudden there I was, smack on the moon, and the gold-colored king was shaking my hand, and saying:

" 'Well, by jinks, if it ain't that Weaver kid—all dressed up fit to kill. Welcome, my boy—welcome to the moon!'

"For a minute, I thought he was making fun of my old ragged clothes—talking about me being all dressed up. But then I saw I was wearing a white shirt, blue pants, and black boots with red tops. I was sure proud.

"Well, almost every night after that, I'd whiz up to the moon. When the moon got small, or even when I couldn't see it at all, I figured it was hidden by clouds, and that I'd have no trouble finding it. And I never did. I'd take off in pitch-darkness, but in a shake of a tail I'd be through the darkness and out where everything was bright. Sometimes I'd rocket around the moon for a while just being glad. Then I'd flip down like a hawk and light on a green lawn, where the king and a lot of kids were always waiting for me. When Ronnie was real little, I used to tell him about the moon. He always wanted me to tell him some more."

"I want to hear more, too," I said. "Tell some of the things you told Ronnie."

Weaver smoothed out another batch of cloth, eyed me suspiciously, saw I was serious, and said:

"I never figured you for a guy who liked kid stuff,

Saxon, but Ronnie sure ate it up. I remember I told him that almost everything was different on the moon—like when you'd go to the store to buy candy, you'd say:

"'Give me a nickel's worth of jawbreakers, please,' and the storekeeper'd put a whole handful of big, shiny black ones in a bag striped red and green and yellow. Then he'd say: 'That will be a nickel.' Then you'd put a nickel on the counter, and the man would say: 'No, no, no. You don't pay for candy on the moon, we pay you.' Then he'd take a nickel from a drawer that had a little bell that rang, and he'd lay the nickel on the counter, and you'd pick it up and go out with your candy, too."

"Fascinating," I said. "What else?"

"Well, I explained that babies on the moon were born old—the boys with whiskers—and that while they grew older, they got younger—and, gosh, a lot of crazy stuff like that."

"Were there buildings on the moon? I mean—like churches, theaters, restaurants, hotels and schools?"

"There were beautiful streets, and red trees, and houses, and big buildings, and churches and schools. There were lots of bicycle stores, and all bicycles cost twenty-five dollars. That is, the bicycle man paid you twenty-five dollars when you bought a bike."

"What about the schools?"

"Well, like I told Ronnie one time, grown-ups who visit the moon have to go to school—start in the first grade. Ronnie loved that part."

"Did you start school on the moon?"

"Well—to tell the truth, I didn't think about school when I went to the moon when I was little. I just made that school part up for Ronnie."

"Weaver," I said, "I've an idea. Could it be that Timmie and Ronnie think you're away from home because you're on a long visit to the moon?"

Weaver looked a bit startled, then said hesitatingly: "Gosh, I don't think so, but it could be."

Trying to keep my voice calm, I said: "Weaver, old son, beginning today, you're on the moon. And what's more, you're starting school there—in the first grade."

Weaver looked at me as if I were slightly crazy. "Now don't get excited," I said, "moon school's not like earth school. No A B C's, for one thing. You see, Weaver, if your boys think you're going to school on the moon, they already know you'll have to start in the first grade. So when you write to them, your letters will have to be written just like a first grade kid would write. Get it?"

"Are you funning me, Saxon?"

"No. I'm not kidding."

"Well, I don't get it. What do you mean—first grade on the moon, and that stuff?"

"Weaver," I said, "I think I've had an answer to prayer, but I'm not sure. Let's skip it until I've had time to think it out."

"Sure," Weaver said. "You know, Saxon—you're a funny guy. Sometimes I wonder if you're not a little nuts."

I awoke next morning with my scheme for Weaver's education fully blown, but it seemed so fantastic that I decided to talk it over with Mr. Williamson before springing it on Weaver; so on the way to work, I stopped at Williamson's office and arranged for him to send for me during the morning. He sent a runner for me at about eleven o'clock, and when I was seated in his office, he said:

"Captain Fowler's excused you from work for an hour. What's on your mind?"

I told him about Weaver's childhood moon fantasies —how each night he'd escaped, in imagination, from the sordid misery and fear in his life to a land where ev-

erything was bright and beautiful—where people loved
each other—where the rules of society were often reversed. I told him about King Golden; the beautiful city
with its red trees; the happy, well-dressed children. Told
him, in fact, everything Weaver'd told me.

Williamson smiled. "Ah, daydreams!" he said. "How
beautifully God helped Weaver find release from the
tensions of his unhappy boyhood."

"Well, sir, I've been thinking like this: Weaver says
they've schools on the moon, and that all grown-ups
who visit the moon start school in the first grade. Now,
why can't I write to Ronnie and Timmie, pretending I'm
King Golden, and tell them their father's visiting on the
moon, so he must start school—in the first grade, of
course. I could explain that since grown-ups on the
moon don't remember what they learned in schools on
the earth, they are really beginning their educations all
over again. I could say their father wants to write to
them from the moon, but that he's afraid they'll be em-
barrassed at receiving letters from a father who's a first-
grader. Then I could ask the boys to encourage their father to write—even though he can only print his letters
at present. It seems to me," I said, "that Weaver'll love
studying as long as he's not being shamed by his ignorance in the eyes of his youngsters. Being able to write
to his kids should make him very happy. Do you understand?"

Williamson chuckled. "Of course I understand. And
I think your plan is an answer to our prayers, Saxon. At
least, it seems to eliminate mental barriers that have
been plaguing Weaver's attempts at schooling. By all
means, try it."

"And it's all right to fool the kids? I mean, well—it's
sort of a lie, isn't it?"

"A lie, my boy, is an untruth told with intent to de-
ceive—a destructive thing. On the other hand, imagina-

tion is a gift of God. It enables the human mind to reach outward and upward. Your moon experiment would probably be called fantasy—and fantasy's merely the youthful form of imagination. Many of our great and worthwhile books are the products of imagination. Many other helpful and entertaining books are the products of fantasy—*Gulliver's Travels* and *Alice in Wonderland* and *Pilgrim's Progress,* for instance. Such books teach valuable lessons—teach in a sort of parable, just as Jesus taught when He told such imaginative stories as 'The Barren Fig Tree,' 'The Lost Sheep,' 'The Lost Coin,' 'The Lost Son,' 'The Wicked Husbandman,' 'The Ten Virgins,' 'The Talents,' and others. My boy, I believe your school on the moon is exactly what a mixed-up man like Weaver needs. And if the experiment succeeds, it will make many happy—Weaver, his wife, his mother, Timmie, Ronnie, you, I, among others. For that reason, if for no other, it's worth a try."

"A few moments ago, Mr. Williamson," I said, "you called it *my* plan. But the basic idea's really Weaver's—I'm only enlarging on what he's already told Ronnie."

"Yes. And that makes it more appropriate. Incidentally, Mr. Osborne, the permanent chaplain here—whose place I'm taking temporarily—has requested extended leave, so I'll be here to watch Weaver's progress. Carry on, my boy."

After work that afternoon I went to the educational department and got six colored pencils—red, blue, green, orange, brown, yellow. That night in my cell I composed a letter to Ronnie and Timmie, illustrating it with small colored drawings—a brown schoolhouse set in a grove of red trees, a man with a long beard studying a book on which was printed 'First Grade Reader,' and things like that. I told the kids that their father'd been on the moon a long time without attending school, and that I'd decided he'd been shilly-shallying long enough; that he must start in the first grade at once. "You know, of course," I wrote, "that only grown-ups go to school here, and that all must start in the lowest grade. Your father isn't very fond of studying and needs encouragement. And that, boys, is why I'm writing to you. Be sure to answer all of his letters promptly. They'll be printed, of course, until he learns 'writing.' Address your letters to Norman Weaver, care of King Golden, Luna City, Moon. Give them to your mother, or grandmother, to mail for you, for they must be posted in a special box." I signed my letter: King Golden.

Next morning, I read the letter to Weaver and explained the plan in more or less detail. At first he seemed to shrink into himself, but when I explained he wouldn't have to attend classes; that I'd teach him in my spare time, he got happily excited and wanted to start right away.

I mailed the letter to Weaver's mother, with an explanatory note, and that night in my cell I printed a short letter, with drawings, for Weaver to copy. It said briefly:

I am going to school on the moon. I am in the first grade. I am learning to print. Soon I will learn to write. King Golden is a kind man. When you buy things on the moon, the store man pays you the price of what you buy. It's all sort of backward here. Please write to me. I will be coming home when I pass into about the third or fourth grade. Kiss Mama and Grandma for me.

Weaver proved handy with a pencil—not only did he copy the letter in good husky print, but he copied the drawing with firmer, more flowing lines than I'd used. I said:

"You've been hiding a light under a bushel, Weaver.

You obviously have a talent for drawing, and you've copied the printed letters perfectly. You're going places, old man."

I had difficulty in getting his copy of the letter away from him. All during work hours, he kept taking it from its envelope and admiring it. But when we passed the yard mailbox after work, he dropped the letter in it himself.

We had an hour before mess, so we hunted a quiet spot in the yard, and I took out my copy of the letter and we began reading lessons. Under a drawing of a full moon, I'd printed: MOON. I spelled the word out for Weaver, he repeated the letters once, and that was that—I never again had to spell the word out for him. Under another drawing I'd printed: SCHOOL. He recognized the two O's at once, and memorized the other letters almost instantly. Under a drawing of a man's head I'd printed: KING. I had a moment of hesitation about spelling that word for him, fearing his reaction to the letter 'G'—but I needn't have worried; he only looked at the letter curiously, and said:

"That's the 'G' I get sick on in school."

"And it doesn't bother you out here in the yard?"

"No—why should it?"

"I don't know," I said, and let it go at that.

I still had five months of my sentence to do when Weaver started school on the moon, and they turned out to be busy months, indeed. Weaver kept urging me to write longer and longer answers to Timmie's and Ronnie's letters—and one or the other of the boys wrote to him nearly every day. After about three months, I started him on script, and he practiced in his cell so persistently that within four weeks he was writing a clear, legible hand. His drawing improved, and I finally persuaded him to begin the prison elementary cartooning course. He'd been writing his own letters for about three weeks when Mr. Williamson wangled him a job in the prison library—distributing returned books to the shelves.

Weaver's letters to his boys became filled with imaginative moon characters and episodes, such as the whale in whose throat was a stairway that led to a room in which were a table, chairs, dish cupboards and bookshelves; the firefly that found Weaver when he was lost, and lighted him home safely; the pug dog that was sad because he looked like a pig; the pig that was sad because he looked like a pug dog—and how they both became happy at last. Delightful fantasies, all.

"Well, that's the story of Weaver's rehabilitation," Saxon said, leaning back in his chair. "But an equally important result of our prayers was what happened to me. In helping Weaver, I forgot myself—with the result that I left prison an entirely new man. Gone was my self-centeredness, my exaggerated sense of my own worth. Instead of feeling responsibility only for myself, I found I'd developed a feeling of responsibility for all with whom I came in contact. I'd asked God to help me help Weaver. God had heard, and had helped me at the same time. Today, I live without worry for the future, and with joy for the opportunities of today. God has been good, indeed."

"And Weaver?"

"Weaver served his full term. Today if you go to a certain city not far from New York, you'll find on one of the main streets, a high-class, efficiently conducted tailor shop. Should you go in, you'll likely be met by a man with a kind, but lined, face—the proprietor."

"Weaver?"

"Yes. And if you show unusual interest in his business, he may tell you that he learned to give customers more than they expect because once upon a time, while he was in prison, he'd helped make going-out clothes for convicts, and had learned how important well-made clothes can be to a man."

"And Timmie and Ronnie?"

"Timmie's studying law. Ronnie's an Air Force pilot. Ruth lives happily with her husband. Weaver's mother is dead now." He went to a filing cabinet, took out a folded letter, opened it and handed it to me. "Weaver's mother wrote that to me not long before she died. Read it."

The letter ended with these words:

. . . and to see my son, a good and proud man, respected by all, and respecting himself, has more than repaid me for whatever sorrow I've had. God be good to you, Marvin Saxon.

AS A BOY I first learned that atheists often pray to God when under severe stress when I heard about an atheist's prayer in the old Chicago Inter-Ocean. In our family, an atheist was thought of as something that wore horns. Consequently, when headlines revealed to me that atheists were as human as the rest of us, I was startled, to say the least. Those headlines read:

ATHEIST'S PRAYER ANSWERED
AS HE CLINGS TO OPEN BRIDGE

The story told how Oscar Hendrikson, chairman of the Illinois Atheists' Forum, while walking along a Chicago street had attempted to step onto a Chicago River bridge just as it began to swing open to let a vessel pass. Hendrikson grasped the end of the bridge as he fell, and was swung out over the center of the stream—hanging by his hands.

In panic, the bridge-tender began to swing the bridge shut again, threatening to crush Hendrikson. Quickly realizing his error, he reversed the motors and once more the bridge swung wide—Hendrikson still hanging by desperately clutching fingers. Unable to swim, Hendrikson feared falling into the water as much as he feared being crushed. He told a reporter later:

"Without realizing I was doing it, I prayed, and it wasn't just an appeal, but a cry for help torn from my very heart. Frightened, despairing, I'd turned to the only power that could save me—a power the existence of which I'd denied since early youth. Here, you see, was a situation where my intelligence was of no use. So spirit

took over, and, of course, did the simple, natural, sensible thing—prayed."

The story went on to tell how a rowboat had put out from a wharf, pulled under Hendrikson and picked him out of the water when he dropped. Three weeks later, in an interview given to a Sunday newspaper, Hendrikson said:

"I couldn't have been hanging from that bridge for more than four or five minutes, but those minutes changed my life. I'd prided myself on being a man of 'pure intellect'—a man above and beyond the rest of humanity, unswayed by feelings—a man who accepted, as fact, only those things that could be proved mathematically or by experiment.

During those fateful minutes, I saw clearly that a man of pure intellect is only partly a man, a useless creature, a sort of thing living in a world he cannot understand and for which he has no sympathy.

"Naturally, my discovery that God is, gave me cause for a deep look at myself. Unable to understand how intellectualism had led me so far astray, I began to wonder if others had been trapped by it, too, so I spent several days reading books on science and philosophy. It was while reading Sir Isaac Newton's Mathematical Principles that I came across a passage I'd heretofore missed. That passage settled for me, once for all, my intellectual doubts about the existence of God. Newton— the scientist who had discovered the laws by which God controls the stars in their courses—said:

" 'It is the dominion of a spiritual being which constitutes God: a true, supreme . . . dominion constitutes a true God. And from His true dominion it follows that the true God is a living, intelligent, and powerful Being; and, for His other perfections, that He is supreme, or most perfect. He is eternal and infinite, omnipotent and omniscient; that is, His duration reaches from eternity* to eternity; His presence from infinity to infinity; He governs all things, and knows all things that are or can be done. He is not eternity and infinity, but eternal and infinite; He is not duration or space, but He endures and is present. He endures forever, and is everywhere present; and by existing always and everywhere, He constitutes duration and space. Since every particle of space is always, and every indivisible moment of duration is everywhere, certainly the Maker and Lord of all things cannot be never and nowhere.'"

That newspaper clipping was filed by my father, who gave it to me for my own scrapbook when I was sixteen. Incidentally, the names of all characters—except those of the four atheists—in the four episodes in the following chapter: "Atheists Pray When the Chips are Down," are true names. I changed the names of the four atheists to save them embarrassment.

Atheists Pray When the Chips are Down

ONE OF THE THINGS I LEARNED FROM MY YEARS OF investigating prayer stories throughout the world is that atheists pray when the chips are down. Another thing I learned is that atheists are usually sheltered men; men who live by the books—thinking other men's thoughts.

Not once during forty years did I find an atheist among men doing the dangerous work of the world; men who build oil lines across desert and mountain, who face wind, sleet, ice and storm to build the communication systems of the earth; men who fight and conquer the perils of the wilderness, who persevere amidst shrieking Arctic blizzards, parching harmattans, hot, sand-cursed siroccos, the furies of Far Pacific typhoons. Nor did I ever meet a gardener who was an atheist.

But I knew one atheist who became a gardener.

His name was Kees Jonker, a Dutch entomologist who was an outspoken atheist. One night he got caught in quicksand in the Ogowe River area of the Cameroons, and lay spread-eagled on his back for half an hour while I worked to get him out. One of the essentials in such situations is that the victim lie quietly, not even speaking, until the rescuer can get a support under him. Even the effort of whispering causes the shoulders to sink more rapidly.

Jonker mumbled and talked during most of the half hour. I finally dragged him to safety after a struggle so strenuous that my ears and nose bled. After my pounding heart had quieted so I could speak, I said to him:

"If you'd not talked so much, Jonker, I'd have had an easier time."

"Sorry," he said. "I wasn't talking; I was praying."

Jonker today is a professor in a large American university. His hobby is flower-gardening. On the pedestal of a large sundial in his garden is a copper plaque on which is engraved this verse of Thomas Brown's:

A garden is a lovesome thing, God wot!
Rose plot,
Fringed pool,
Fern'd grot—
The veriest school
Of peace; and yet the fool
Contends that God is not—
Not God! in gardens! When the eve is cool?
Nay, but I have a sign:
'Tis very sure God walks in mine.

Professor Horace Schroeder, like Professor Jonker, was an entomologist and an atheist. At Elizabethville, in the Congo, he joined a party of Protestant and Catholic missionaries that was headed for the Ubangi-Shari country, where Schroeder had an appointment to meet a Chinese biologist. When the missionaries prayed before meals, Schroeder would make such remarks as:

"Prayer is the refuge of the ignorant. Prayer is superstition."

The missionaries ignored his remarks, but they didn't like them.

In Africa, the most deadly snake is the black mamba, a member of the cobra family, but not hooded. It's not unusual to find black mambas that measure eleven or twelve feet long. Because the black mamba travels with the lower half of its body on the ground and the top half reared high so that it can see above top of the grass, it's often called "the-snake-that-walks-on-its-tail." Usually all that one sees of a mamba is its black venomous head moving above waving grasses. When one passes you, it glares with an evil-looking black eye, and flickers a black tongue.

A black mamba's venom is so deadly that few humans live for more than one hour after being bitten. The black mamba is so fast that in one instance—officially verified by the British Army—the snake chased an officer on horseback and killed him. The black mamba's strike is powerful. Oom Paul Kruger, first president of the Transvaal Republic, tells of a mamba that, after knocking down a fifteen-year-old boy, leaped among the men of a patrol he was leading against the British. He bit three more men and then turned on two dogs, chasing and biting them. Boy, men and dogs died in less than half an hour. The mamba got away.

Schroeder knew about mambas.

One morning as the missionary party prepared to

walk single file along a narrow ledge on the side of a
red, rocky hill called a *kopje,* Schroeder in the lead, the
rest of the party trailing behind him, a boulder dislodged
by a baboon rolled and bounded down the slope, dis-
turbing a nest of black mambas. One, a large olive-black
male, slithered off an outcropping and coiled angrily on
the ledge just in front of Schroeder.

For a long minute the snake and the atheist faced
one another—the mamba's glittering eyes almost level
with Schroeder's, its black forked tongue flickering, its
neck swelling with anger. Schroeder, within a split
second of death, *prayed* so loudly that the frightened
mamba actually sailed over low bushes and rocks in its
headlong flight downhill.

After Schroeder had calmed down a bit, he looked
around, smiled and said sheepishly:

"I prayed, didn't I?"

"Of course you did, son," a missionary said.

In the Adamawa Highlands of the Cameroons, men
still laugh about the atheistic Scots archeologist who became a mighty prayer because he thought, mistakenly,
that he was about to be devoured by cannibals.

His name was Duncan Featherstonewall, and he'd
been captured in the N'Djole country by the one-time
cannibalistic Fan tribe. They'd picked Featherstonewall
up because, after watching him roaming about the
country digging holes with his pick and shovel, they'd
concluded he was a magician intent on doing them
harm.

Within an hour of his capture, the Fans dispatched a
runner to Duola with a request to authorities that they
"take the white wizard away." White hunter Juan Feliz
was sent to get him.

Meanwhile, Featherstonewall, with feet bound, sat on
the ground and watched women of the tribe fill a large

cast-iron kettle with water, then build a fire under it.
The women, half frightened, half curious, kept glancing
covertly at Featherstonewall, and those glances convinced him that they were planning to cook him. Actually, the women were preparing to cook two small
goats.

Feliz arrived to conduct Featherstonewall back to
civilization just as the "atheist" had begun frantic pleas
to God to save him from the fancied peril. Feliz later
said:

"Featherstonewall was roaring prayers for help in
both English and Afrikaans. His appeals were so loud
that the women were frightened from their cooking pot.
And although I told him he'd been in no danger, he
never believed me."

That was many years ago, yet Featherstonewall—
still an archeologist two years ago when I last heard of
him—was still a praying man.

The following story of the conversion of an atheist
was told me by a Dutch Reformed Church minister
named Hans de Hooch. Years later, when I met anthro-
pologist Karl Karls in Liverpool, he verified the episode.

"Karls and I," De Hooch said, "joined a party headed by a famous African guide named Nicobar Jones,
who was leaving Kimberley to search for the Soares
party, long overdue at Chukudu Kraal in the heart of
the Kalahari Desert. Karls was on a trip to collect Hottentot relics. I was going along as a minister, in order to
render such spiritual aid as I could to the Soares party
in case we found them in extremities. Jones warned
Karls that the journey would likely be an agonizing one,
but that didn't discourage him.

"Karls was so placid a fellow that one day when the
subject of prayer came up, it surprised me to have him
lose his equilibrium. He said testily:

" 'Persons who pray in emergencies, De Hooch, do so because they lack self-confidence. A truly capable man doesn't need prayer.' Then hastily he added: 'Sorry. It always annoys me to find people relying on God instead of themselves.'

"The desert was the driest it had been in twelve years. Even the usual brackish pools in dry river beds had evaporated. Only the Bushmen could locate any water, and we were glad we had two of those marvelous little desert travelers in our outfit."

The Kalahari is almost pure red, or pure white, sand. During even the driest years, Bushmen find water, but in such small quantities that sometimes an entire day is required to fill a two-quart canteen. In some areas during unusually dry years, only the water-impregnated roots of gourds and tubers makes life possible.

The Kalahari is covered with knee-high grass tufts that get so dry that the leaves crumble to tinder at a touch. Great areas of that desert are covered also with bushes, each so like the others that none is outstanding enough to be used as a landmark. It's not uncommon for even the Bushmen to get lost in such seas of monotony as those bush-covered areas are.

"After a nightmarish journey of endless days of thirst, heat and drifting sands," De Hooch continued, "we found the Soares party—all of them dead, including the kaffirs—tongues swollen, nostrils and lips split from dryness, vulture picked, jackal mauled.

"As you know, water in the Kalahari usually lies atop a thin, brittle layer of packed sand about six feet down. We found that the Soares party had dug a deep hole with their hands, and that water had begun seeping onto the brittle layer—but too slowly for such thirst-crazed humans. Evidently hoping to get a faster flow, they had broken through the water-retaining crust, only to have their hope of life—water—drain off and down to the sands below.

"We covered the pitiful group with sand, feeling pretty low, for by then we knew that our searching party had reached the point of no return. Our canteens were empty and our two Bushmen hadn't been able to locate even one drop of water during the past sixteen hours. That meant we had only eight hours left—for in desert country, twenty-four hours without water is man's limit. But we had to go on, and we did—heat-burned feet, split lips, swollen eyes, dry skin itch—almost beyond endurance. We plodded on and on, deceived by heartbreaking mirages of cool falling waters and wind-rippled pools.

"Came sunset, and still no water. I told Karls that this night might well be our last. He didn't answer, just stood staring into the molten-copper western sky. Then, mumbling through parched lips, he staggered a little way apart, and knelt, apparently praying. He knelt a long while and seemed to be still praying when I fell asleep.

"Shortly after midnight, a party of Bushmen women carrying six ostrich-egg shells filled with water came across us. And the amount of precious water that they gave us proved exactly enough to see us through the rest of our way—to the well at Chukudu.

"That evening, Karls said to me:

"Something drove me to my knees, predikant De Hooch. And when those women arrived with water, I *knew* I was no longer an atheist.'"

In the early 1920's, while I was in Burke, Idaho, to get the stories of twelve miners who'd been rescued miraculously after a cave-in in the Hecla mine, someone asked me why I didn't get the prayer story of Weldon Connor—"that old atheist."

"An atheist with a prayer answer?" I said.

"Well, he isn't an atheist any more, since he fell off the cliff. But he used to startle folks by declaring: 'If there *is* a God, I challenge Him to strike me dead here and now.' He became quite a drinking man, and the more he drank, the more often he'd roar at God to 'strike me dead.'"

"And falling off a cliff cured his atheism?" I asked.

"Yes. But go and ask Connor about it. It's quite a story, and he tells it well."

I located Connor in a miner's shack about two miles out of Burke, toward Mullan. He was a weathered old fellow with gnarled hands, a pug nose and black, overhanging eyebrows. His hair was gray.

"Sure I'll tell you about my miracle," he said, and invited me to sit at an oilcloth-covered kitchen table. "I used to be an atheist," he began, "thought I was proving something when I used to defy God—if there was a God—to strike me down."

"I know about that," I said.

"Playing kid games, that was. Now I know that God don't play kid games with anybody. Well, one morning in early spring while there was still snow under logs and on top of shaded boulders, I went up the mountain behind my shack to see if I could shoot a bear. I trailed the bear to a cliff, stepped onto the snowcap, and the cap slid over the brink like it was greased—and me with it. It wasn't much of a fall—about forty feet, maybe —but I lit on the end of my spine, and at the same time, my rifle fell, muzzle first, on the back of my neck. Between them two bumps, I was paralyzed from the neck down—couldn't move a hand or a foot.

"The fall was bad enough by itself, but I'd fallen into a big wooden wheel—a pulley eighteen feet across. This pulley was horizontal to the ground, and from rim to hub it had four six-inch-square spokes. The pulley rested on a wooden foundation to which two eight-inch-square beams were spiked. Lumbermen call that foundation a platform. An axle ran up from the platform, through the hub of the pulley, and when the pulley turned, its big spokes cleared the beams on the platform by just about one inch. The spokes and the beams were like big shears.

"Now, I was lying up against one of the platform beams, and one of the pulley spokes was within one foot of my stretched-out body. If that pulley had turned just a couple of feet, I'd have been cut in half, lengthwise.

"Two belts—steel ropes—ran around the rim of the pulley, one to a big cable drum, the other in the opposite direction, to a small pulley on a donkey engine. When the donkey engine was running, the big pulley turned slowly, winding up the cable on the drum. The other end of the cable was fastened to a log down in the canyon. The idea was to pull the logs up the slope to a flat where they could be handled.

"Well, sir, there I was, lying hidden and helpless, inside the pulley. And all of a sudden, I heard voices at the donkey engine. Two men were getting ready to start it. I yelled as best I could—which wasn't much—but they didn't hear me. I tell you, mister, I was in a state. In minutes—seconds, maybe—I'd be scissored lengthways like a halved beef. I was screaming inside myself while I tried, with all I had, to move—and couldn't. Then I heard that donkey engine start, and I began to pray.

"'God,' I said, sweat running in my eyes, 'don't let them open the throttle—don't let them open the throttle.' Then I thought: You asked God to strike you dead many times, Connor. Maybe this is the way He's going to take you up on it. Well, sir, I sort of quieted down. And I prayed again: 'I never did mean it, God—I was only acting smart. Don't hold my kid game against me, God. I don't want to die. Help me, God.'

"Well, mister, right then, the engine's tone got deeper, and I knew the throttle had been pulled. I shut my eyes—and the miracle happened!

"My rifle had fallen against the spoke I was right next to. I'd been carrying it with the safety off and the bolt back, expecting to meet that bear any moment. And why that gun didn't go off when it lit on my head, I don't know—but it didn't. And when the wheel began to turn, that old rifle exploded with a roar. You see, the trigger'd caught on a big splinter on the spoke, and when the pulley had moved about half an inch, the gun fired. Now, here's an astonishing thing: I don't think by this time, those men could have stopped me from being crushed even if they'd tried. But God did. You see, *the bullet shot the magneto right off the engine!"*

"But, Connor," I said, "the rifle fell just right. Even if you hadn't prayed, the thing would have happened."

"No," he said, "it wouldn't have happened. You see, mister, while I was praying—shaking my head in desperation—my head bumped the rifle, moving it just barely enough to hang the trigger guard on that splinter. If I *hadn't* prayed so desperately, I wouldn't have been shaking my head so hard. And if I'd moved my head only a quarter-of-an-inch less, they'd have buried me in two pieces."

"And now you're a praying man," I said.

"Yes. Wouldn't you be—if that had happened to you?"

"Yes, Connor, I would," I said.